"Good routines can propel us forward as a way to ... changing habits. John Brandon has made the case for using simple daily practices to transform how you live your life."

Nir Eyal, bestselling author of *Indistractable*

"Productivity is all about habits: forming and nurturing the beneficial ones, recognizing and ditching the harmful ones. Brandon's book teaches you how to build (and stick to) a set of daily routines for staying focused and motivated. It doesn't matter what kind of person you are—lazy, hyperactive, distracted, overachieving—this book will work for everyone. It's like a skeleton key for unlocking the human brain's potential."

Michael Calore, senior editor of *WIRED*

"Anyone in business knows time is a precious commodity. What John Brandon has done in his new book is offer practical guidance on how to focus our attention and use time wisely. It's a game changer for those seeking a competitive advantage."

Jason Feifer, editor-in-chief of *Entrepreneur*

"In our world of information overload, *The 7-Minute Productivity Solution* provides a much-needed fresh perspective on navigating all of the pulls on our attention so we can actually feel fulfilled at the end of the day. John's humor and wit makes this a fun read with incredibly valuable tips to improve performance and overall well-being."

Kristel Bauer PA-C, founder of Live Greatly

"John Brandon has pulled off a not-so-small miracle here: he's written a book about daily routines that's a page-turner. He makes the quotidian exotic and turns everyday habits into superpowers. Any one of the nine 7-minute routines in this book will change how you work and, even more, how much you enjoy your work. But all nine routines together? Prepare, as far as your output goes, to become a machine. Prepare, as far as your heart goes, to become more truly, fully, and deeply human. My only critique of John Brandon is he didn't write *The 7-Minute Productivity Solution* twenty years ago. Oh, the things I might have done and the joy I could have had doing them. But so be it: I have the book now, and, well, so do you. Get ready. Your most outlandish dreams and farfetched goals are about to become not only doable but almost inevitable. Get ready to transform."

Mark Buchanan, author of *God Walk: Moving at the Speed of Your Soul*

"When I started out, I asked a famous writer for advice: How was she able to publish bestsellers year after year? Her answer: *sitzfleisch*, a Yiddish-German word that means, roughly, 'butt in the seat.' She wakes up, goes straight to her desk, and writes five hundred words. Every day. In nine months, she completes a book, goes on tour, then starts over. I never really understood how this was possible until reading John Brandon's inspiring and practical approach to productivity with purpose. John provides the 7-minute strategies each of us need to make *sitzfleisch* joyful and meaningful."

Michael Heller, Columbia Law School professor and coauthor of *Mine!*

"*The 7-Minute Productivity Solution* is bite-sized and gospel-centric. A great read!"

Jordan Raynor, national bestselling author of *Redeeming Your Time*

"Are you distracted by many things? Do you have more on your 'to do' list than you can ever get done? Are you high-performing yet feel like you could be even more productive if you could get a handle on the ever-multiplying demands of social media and digital communication? John Brandon offers real, concise, immediately applicable help in just seven minutes! Too good to be true? The investment you make in reading this book will return to you manyfold in the increased productivity you will experience and the bonus of deriving greater joy in each accomplished task."

Carmen LaBerge, host of *Mornings with Carmen*, author of *Speak the Truth*, and curator of ReconnectwithCarmen.com

"John Brandon has a God-given gift of connecting the dots between what matters most and what matters now. If you want to develop good productivity habits, this book is a must-read. John's years of practice, successes, and research will inspire and help anyone make the most of their time—the most precious of gifts."

Brittany Thoms, owner of See.Spark.Go

"John Brandon's book is filled with incredibly powerful yet exceedingly doable insights for achieving productivity with purpose. And it is a joy to read. This is a welcome resource on managing your schedule and obtaining outstanding results in a sustainable way. Use this book as a guide to begin creating new and better productivity routines today."

Matt Perman, director of career development at The King's College and author of *What's Best Next*

"In this book, John Brandon provides motivation, evidence-based explanations, and practical steps to help us make the best use of our time, our resources, and our opportunities."

Paul Jorgensen, church planter and former pastor of Cornerstone Church, Minnesota

"As the pastor and CEO of a thriving church, the father of a busy eight-year-old, and the owner of several businesses, the question I'm often asked is, 'How do you stay sane in the chaos?' For years my answer has always been the same: 'With God's help.' And that is still true. But it is also known that God helps those who help themselves. And after reading my dear friend John Brandon's book, *The 7-Minute Productivity Solution*, I have adjusted my response. John's book teaches that the task you are working on should actually be the task you want to complete. Calibrating your day is much more productive than surviving your day. One of the most profound excerpts of this book is the 7-minute morning routine: prepare, clear your head, read a little, and write notes. If you're busy like me, and you're trying to figure out a way to make it all happen, this book is for you."

Keion Henderson, pastor of The Lighthouse
Church of Houston

The
7-Minute
Productivity
Solution

The
7-Minute
Productivity
Solution

How to Manage Your Schedule, Overcome Distraction, and Achieve the Results You Want

JOHN BRANDON

Revell

a division of Baker Publishing Group
Grand Rapids, Michigan

© 2022 by John Brandon

Published by Revell
a division of Baker Publishing Group
PO Box 6287, Grand Rapids, MI 49516-6287
www.revellbooks.com

Printed in the United States of America

Library of Congress Cataloging-in-Publication Data
Names: Brandon, John, 1965– author.
Title: The 7-minute productivity solution : how to manage your schedule,
    overcome distraction, and achieve the results you want / John Brandon.
Other titles: The Seven minute productivity solution
Description: Grand Rapids, MI : Revell, a division of Baker Publishing Group,
    2022. |
Identifiers: LCCN 2021020275 | ISBN 9780800740252 (paperback) | ISBN
    9780800741389 (casebound) | ISBN 9781493434398 (ebook)
Subjects: LCSH: Time management. | Distraction (Psychology) | Motivation
    (Psychology) | Self-actualization (Psychology)
Classification: LCC HD69.T54 B73 2022 | DDC 650.1/1—dc23
LC record available at https://lccn.loc.gov/2021020275

Published in association with the Hartline Literary Agency, LLC.

Baker Publishing Group publications use paper produced from sustainable forestry
practices and post-consumer waste whenever possible.

22 23 24 25 26 27 28   7 6 5 4 3 2 1

To my kids:
Rachel
Hannah
Josh
Katie

Contents

Contents

Acknowledgments

WRITING A BOOK is an exercise in extreme productivity.

It's not just doing the research, developing the structure, and writing the words. It's about the perseverance needed to stick with the plan. I often relied on coffee to help me type faster (imagine a highly caffeinated gerbil and you'll get the picture) and then had to dig deep for inner motivation.

Over an eighteen-month period, I spent many long hours reading books and articles, writing down notes in a journal, and following my own routines. Productivity is both a decision and a mindset. Most of us don't suddenly become productive but develop good productivity habits over time.

Writing a book tests that concept like no other. If the habits you need to write a book have not already developed—for example, you keep looking at your phone to read text messages from your kids or you choose an Xbox controller over a keyboard—you won't make it past chapter 1.

That's why it was so fun to look back and think about the people who helped me write this book. These are the folks who pushed me forward one step at a time, reminded me about the deeper purpose behind this endeavor, and even brought over a cup of coffee when needed.

My agent, Jim Hart, really made the dream come true. His industry connections, attention to detail, and constant encouragement made it all possible from day one. On day two, it was Vicki Crumpton, executive editor at Revell. What a wonderful collaborator during the initial proposal stages and all the way through to the final revisions. The entire team at Revell acted in a spirit of shared unity and vision. Without them, this book would have never materialized. I'm also indebted to my early readers and researchers: Rachel, Katie, Jade, Annie, Ellie, Chyelle, Richard, Kaylyn, Stephen, Joe, Shayna, Ginny, Linsey, and Collin.

Productivity also has a geographic element. I hunkered down at the Wilderness Fellowship Prayer Cabins in a remote part of Wisconsin several times, often without a reliable internet connection—thank you, Lord. I sequestered myself in hotels and at regional parks, ordering my food by DoorDash and snacking on beef jerky. The silence and reflection I experienced at the King's House in Buffalo, Minnesota, helped me stay focused.

Authors Mark Buchanan, Jordan Raynor, Nir Eyal, Cal Newport, Ryder Carroll, Bob Goff, Chris Bailey, Matt Perman, and many others were my constant companions, at the least in how I lugged their books around but also when I emailed them and chatted by phone. I'm forever grateful to Mark Buchanan, one of my all-time favorite authors, because he said really nice things about my early manuscript and inspired me to persevere.

Over thirty-four years of married life, one person fanned my flame of productivity the most. We go on hikes in the dark woods, talking about future plans and watching as they come to fruition, wide-eyed with wonder. We debate our life decisions together, praying in the early morning hours until we have clear, God-ordained answers. My life would not be the same without my wife, Rebecca, and neither would this book. Along the way, my adult kids and their spouses have become my beacons of hope. Rachel (and Jonas), Hannah (and Eddie), Joshua, and Katie (and Blake), you're all great gifts.

Finally, I owe everything to my Lord and Savior Jesus Christ, who gave me the words and helped me find favor. As it says in Proverbs 16:9 (NIV): "In their hearts humans plan their course, but the LORD establishes their steps" and, as it turns out, helped me write this book.

Introduction

The secret of your future is hidden in your daily
routine. —Mike Murdock

I **WAS WORRIED** about my laptop.

There I was, walking on a frozen lake in Minnesota as the
sun arced above the horizon. In the morning light, I looked like
outdoorsman Bear Grylls with a fuzzy beard and wool hat. I could
have driven my car across the ice, but where's the fun in that?
Still, I didn't want to waste time. Ahead of me, I could see my
destination: a private island about a mile away. My friend told
me I could use his cabin, and I intended to make every second
count. My laptop wasn't exactly durable, and the temperature
was below freezing.

That's when I glanced at my watch. It was 7:00 a.m., and breakfast was calling my name. I quickly calculated how long my walk
would take. *You're gonna make it*, I told myself a few times. Behind
me, I pulled a sled packed with the essentials: a sleeping bag, food,
an extra pair of boots.

The first thing I noticed when I reached the cabin was that the
snow had built up a wall around it, making it seem like my own
private fortress. Cool! I typed in a code to open the door and set
down my backpack and other gear.

I still remember how cold the laptop felt. I imagined it had "bricked" during my winter trek. I grabbed a few chunks of wood and built a fire in the fireplace, boiled some eggs, set up a temporary office space, and took a seat at the table. With a sigh of relief, I heard my computer come to life.

I was about to start writing my first book, but before connecting to the hotspot on my phone and opening my word processor, I decided to do something I've done almost every day for the last twenty years.

My fingers were a bit stiff, but I cracked open a journal and grabbed a pen. *Prepare the work area*, I reminded myself. I pushed aside a flashlight and box of matches, ordered the space in front of me, and straightened my chair. I set my watch down on the table and stashed my phone in a zippered compartment. *Breathe a little in and out, for exactly one minute*, I thought. As the sun broke through the trees, I listened to the fire crackle next to me and felt the warmth on my legs. *Write down your thoughts for the day but avoid making a complete list of everything.* What's making me feel stressed and worried? What is giving me hope? How do my tasks match up with my purpose?

Lastly, I looked over the notes I had written and circled the most important one: *write a chapter of the book.* I was ready to start working.

It's a simple routine, but I remember feeling relaxed and calm. As a writer, my most important accessories are my fingers. They were primed and ready to type. As the wind died down and I thought about cooking up a steak for lunch, I cranked out an entire chapter in one sitting.

Why We Need Routines

Routines help us form new habits.

When we wake up in the morning, we shower, brush our teeth, and comb our hair. That's a personal hygiene habit. At work, we start up our computer, open a browser, and check email. That habit helps us dive into work quickly. I'm easily distracted and have multiple "squirrel moments" throughout the day, so I need routines to guide me, such as the journaling I did at the cabin that morning.

Journaling is one of several routines I'll explain in this book. Writing in a journal each morning helps you collect your thoughts so that you become more intentional with your time. Ending your day with a personal daily debriefing is a routine that helps you evaluate what you accomplished and why. There's even a routine to help you take a break more efficiently. Coffee optional.

In all these routines, you'll learn how to be efficient with your time and how to match *what you do* with *what you care about*.

The opposite of that? It's not anything good. The second half of this book explains what happens when bad habits like social media obsession keep us from achieving what is meaningful and desirable.

The opposite of a routine is a deep rut leading us nowhere— also known as a bad habit. You might struggle with checking email too often or browsing the web all day at work. Been there, done that! A rut is a slow and agonizing slog in the wrong direction to reach unimportant goals.

When we feel stressed, tired, and hungry—when life happens— a routine helps us get back on course. Author Greg McKeown says it best: "The right routines give us the equivalent of an energy rebate. Instead of spending our limited supply of discipline on making the same decisions again and again, embedding our decisions into a routine allows us to channel that discipline toward some other essential activity."[1]

∿∿∿

Back at the island, I closed my computer. There's a sense of well-being that comes when we complete tasks. I started a fire outside and cooked up a late-night stew. In my journal, I started a daily debrief session. *Write down your biggest accomplishment of the day.* That was easy, I wrote an entire chapter of a book and didn't burn myself near the fire (outdoor cooking is not my forte). *Write down your biggest stressors.* Getting to the island wasn't easy. I thought I had destroyed my laptop. *Note whether your activities matched up with your long-term goals.* That was also easy. I was writing a book. It had been a lifelong dream until then.

After my debrief, I slipped into a bunk bed and dozed off. The routines that day set me on a path toward good productivity.

Routines set a tone for efficiency, helping you develop good habits that last your entire life.

A good habit means you're driving in the fast lane. Buckle up and hold on for the ride! You'll reach your destination quickly and efficiently.

A bad habit means you're in the slow lane or, worse, stuck on the side of the road. Constant distractions and derailments keep you from making progress. The philosopher William James once wrote, "The more of the details of our daily life we can hand over to the effortless custody of automatism, the more our higher powers of mind will be set free for their own proper work."[2]

This book gives you nine helpful routines to either jump-start your productivity or rid yourself of bad habits. You need to invest only seven minutes in each routine. That's it! If you follow these routines, you'll focus on what's most important and become a highly productive person.

More importantly, you'll experience what I call *productivity with purpose.* As author and marketing expert Ryan Holiday notes, "A good routine is not only a source of great comfort and stability, it's the platform from which stimulating and fulfilling work is possible."[3]

〰〰

Before we go further, here's something to think about: scientists have found we can pay close attention to something for about five to ten minutes before our brains start to lose focus and switch off like a light bulb.[4] (I've split the difference and made each routine seven minutes long.)

You might be listening to a school lecture, watching a presentation by one of your coworkers, or checking email. After seven minutes, your brain needs to hit pause. The neurons slow down when we focus for too long. That's why I'm only asking for a short period of time to follow the routines. The routines are intentionally basic to help you maintain focus.

You can also follow the routines at any time or place during the day—say, in a cabin in the middle of nowhere or at your desk before a meeting. You can follow them at home or on a plane flying across the world. You can follow them on the bus or in the car, which might sound like the book *Green Eggs and Ham* but just go with it—the routines work! I know this because I've been using them for years. Focusing your attention on *one thing* for only seven minutes minimizes distraction. Mix and match the routines that work best for you, and don't worry about doing them all.

You'll increase productivity, but you'll also free up more of your time so that you can put more effort into the things that really matter.

Productivity with Purpose

My journey to *productivity with purpose* started with a major career change. I used to be a corporate manager, but my wife suggested I start a writing career instead. I became a full-time writer back in 2001.

My wife encouraged me to follow my passion—not to mention use my journalism degree!—for more purposeful work. Since then, I've written reports for Fox News about protecting kids online,[5] interviewed famous people such as Francis Chan[6] and Andy Stanley,[7] and once wrote a story about a church that started a unique community-service project.[8] In my columns, I've written about productivity and work-life balance most often.

Work is part of what makes us human. It helps us find meaning in life, serve others, and become part of something bigger than ourselves. The alternative to work is to live like a slug, burning away our lives in meaningless pursuits, also called *watching television.*

It's not a question of whether we should work and toil; it's *how we work* and *what we are trying to accomplish in life* that's important.

Once we see work as a meaningful pursuit and part of what it means to be human, it's much easier to set aside the need for constant success and recognition. Working hard is wired into our DNA. We may no longer be plowing a field by hand, but we do understand that work is a noble effort. Our productivity can involve a marketing campaign in the office, school papers at home with our kids, or building a major corporation.

Since we are wired as humans to work hard and find satisfaction in toil and labor, we can rest easy. We already have the impulse and longing to achieve great things. We don't need to prove our value, since the value is intrinsic simply because we're human. We can set aside a need for constant success when we realize that. We breathe, we eat, we work.

Even if you're already productive, you can learn from the routines in this book. Improve all of us we can, as the wise sage Yoda might say.

We all have twenty-four hours in a day. We all breathe about twenty thousand times per day.[9] We all have about fifty to seventy thousand thoughts per day.[10] We're all in this together, struggling to learn and grow and become better at what we do. The important question is, What will you do with your twenty-four hours, twenty thousand breaths, and fifty thousand thoughts? Where will they lead you?

〜〜〜

As I was researching habit formation for this book and how people become productive and successful, I discovered a few themes.

I read all the best authors, including Adam Grant, Nir Eyal, James Clear, and Dan Heath. They kept stressing the same things: habits form when we follow a predetermined routine. The best routine leads to the best results. Think about driving a car. First, you learn to use the gas pedal and the brakes, then you learn to drive. Eventually, stepping on the gas and the brakes becomes second nature. We don't have to think about it. But when we multitask, we end up losing focus. Look out! You haven't quite mastered the brakes yet! Habits also make us who we are. That's quite scary if your habits involve smoking cigarettes or playing video games all day. Yet, once you learn to drive, you can go places. Such as Chipotle.

Some of the routines I'll cover in each section are similar to those in other productivity books, but the twist is that they are about more than just becoming a better person and developing more skills. The goal is *to become who we were meant to be all along*. The goal is to do our work with this in mind: we were created for work as humans. We may sweat and toil all day, but we do so with integrity, honor, and a clear focus.

As author Mark Buchanan once told me, "We're always having to justify what we do on some hidden scale of values. This is not a bad thing. But there is another reason to be productive: I am productive because I am made in the image of God. If I deny that, I am denying the Almighty."[11]

Tim Keller writes about this in his book *Every Good Endeavor*: "If God's purpose for your job is that you serve the community, then the way to serve God best is to do the job as well as it can be done."[12]

My Own Story

I wasn't always so productive and purposeful. In my younger years, I was easily bored and didn't know basic productivity techniques.

The radical shift in my work habits occurred when I started writing as a journalist full-time. In the last twenty years, I've written fifteen thousand articles for major publications such as *Inc.*, *Forbes*, *Popular Mechanics*, *Wired*, and *Entrepreneur*. There are few full-time journalists working today who match my total output over these last twenty years with such a diverse roster of publications. That's not a humble brag. It's remarkable to me and a credit to my faith and dependence on God as well as the techniques in this book.

My greatest burst of productivity started in 2008 when I wrote a daily online column for *Inc.* Over a decade, I wrote four thousand columns on leadership, mentoring, technology, and other topics, sometimes posting twice per day (for those who are questioning the math). All told, about a half million people followed my column every month.

That means around *sixty million people* have read my daily business column at Inc.com and in the magazine since 2008. That total doesn't include writing for Forbes.com or a long-standing weekly column for FoxNews.com that also dates back to 2008. I've written thousands of articles for many other outlets as well. I can juggle, cook pancakes, and recite poetry at the same time too. Not really, and maybe I've taken this too far, but honestly, I'm remarkably efficient. I've written at least a dozen articles about Elon Musk alone!

One highlight came in 2015 when I wrote about the seven-minute morning routine for Inc.com.[13] To my own surprise and excitement, the article went viral. To date, two million people have read that simple guide to having a morning routine, and thousands of people are already following my format. This book is a result of watching how that morning routine has helped so many people become productive.

I mention all of this with wide-eyed bewilderment. I needed a calculator to figure this out, but over a twenty-year span I've estimated a total production of around *eighteen million words* with an average of about one thousand words per article. You can google almost all of them if you want. It's astounding to me.*

∿∿∿

People often ask me how this is possible. I usually say, "It's my job."

And yet, applying the productivity lessons in this book will save time, improve your own process, produce better results, and even help you lead a more fulfilled life. A routine is the engine to help you *actually* develop new habits—starting today. There is a method to this madness. If we are designed to work, we should steward that work as best we can.

There are times when I hear about extreme productivity and nod along in agreement. "That's me, that's how I work." Yet some of the productivity advice I've found has left me feeling a little flat. Is that all there is? Getting better as a person? Small changes in self-improvement? Becoming more successful, so you can make more money? There must be more to it.

In researching this book, I felt as if the natural laws of habit forming and personal development were not satisfying. I don't want to be *merely* a better person. I don't want to be an email guru; I don't even like email. I decided the real reason for becoming more efficient is because that honors who we are as humans. We are *good workers* at heart. I choose to become intentional with my time because my time on this planet is limited.

---

* Following is a list of publications that have published my articles since 2001: Inc.com, Forbes.com, *Wired, Popular Mechanics, Entrepreneur,* TechRadar, *Popular Science, Computerworld,* CIO.com, CIO Insights, The Ladders, *Business News Daily, Business 2.0,* CSO, FoxNews.com, *Chicago Tribune, Outside, Men's Journal, New Man, Christianity Today, Paste, Relevant Magazine,* TechHive.com, *PC Magazine, PC World,* CIO Traction Watch, VentureBeat.com, Baseline, *Breakaway, Campus Life, InSite Magazine, Alliance Life, Beacon, Coastal Living, Computer Shopper, Macworld, MacUser UK, PC Plus Magazine, Windows Magazine, Linux Format, Shutterbug, Digital Photo Pro Magazine,* GamesRadar.com, Games Domain.com, GameZone.com, *Electronic Gaming Monthly, How It Works,* Gizmodo, *Laptop, PC Upgrade, Tech Edge, MIT Technology Review.*

As purposeful workers, we don't have to follow the same old routines and habits. Each day, we can create new habits and break old ones. Starting right now we can say, *Today, I will work hard. Today, I will embrace change. Today, I will start using new routines to form new habits.*

One day at a time. One routine at a time.

You *can* become more purposeful in your work. You can look back and say you made the most of the resources at your disposal. You can match your tasks to your purpose. You can make good decisions about how to live.

And if you make a mistake—well, you can start again tomorrow.

Here's the thing about *productivity with purpose*. The emphasis is on the *purpose*. We work hard, we manage our time, we take great comfort in the fact that we have labored for good reason and for good outcomes.

We're ready to begin a journey not of mere self-development but to experience a more fulfilling and rewarding life and to become more productive because that's how we were created: to work with joy. Are you ready? Buckle up for the ride. We're going to put the pedal to the metal by starting with the morning routine that helped me write my first book in a cabin long ago.*

---

* In case you're wondering, I applied the same routines to write this book as well. I even went back to the island—in the summertime.

PART 1

Develop Good Habits

Morning Routine

You'll never change your life until you change something you do daily. The secret of your success is found in your daily routine.

—JOHN MAXWELL

1

Define What Is Meaningful

IT WAS THE BIGGEST FAILURE of my life. On September 18, 2001—just a week after 9/11—I lost my job. I was a corporate manager and drove forty-five minutes to work one way in heavy commuter traffic. I wore a tie and wing-tipped shoes. I managed a large staff, including web designers and writers. I was on the fast track at a consumer electronics company destined to become a vice president and lead an entire department.

Then it all came crashing down.

I came into work and my boss escorted me to a conference room with a handful of lawyers and some legal papers to sign. Not good. The economy was sinking faster than a bag of bricks in a swimming pool. I had to agree to a severance package and leave that same day . . . or else. My boss ushered me to the front entrance and took my security card.

"Sorry we had to do this to you," he said, looking a bit grim.

Let's just say it was a long drive home.

The next morning, I woke up at dawn. With four little kids at home, two of them barely out of diapers, I knew I had to act quickly. The house payment was due, and my oldest daughter needed braces. I thought about seeking legal help and realized that was probably a dead end.

At the kitchen table, I sat down with a journal and a pen and wrote out my worst fears, deepest regrets, and biggest dreams. *Will I ever write a book? Can I do ministry with students someday? Why was I the first to be let go in the downsizing?* I jotted down a note about wanting more out of my career. I still have those faded sheets of paper in a well-worn journal.

I decided to write down my thoughts every morning. It was my only avenue for dealing with the deep disappointment of losing my job, of failing in a way that was so obvious to my friends and family. I haven't collected a regular paycheck in a corporate job since, and I'll explain more of my story later, but what really came out of that experience is this book. Roughly fifteen thousand articles and twenty years later, my biggest failure led to my greatest workplace success.

You see, I decided to become a writer that day.

Actually, my wife, Rebecca, suggested the idea. She knew I had a degree in journalism. She knew I had a deep longing to share my own thoughts and ideas, to put words on a page, to make a living as a professional author. She knew I wasn't happy being a director in an information technology department. (I might have constantly complained about it.) That day, I not only started writing in a journal to organize my thoughts, I started writing as a career.

I cobbled together enough income to support my family. Well, almost. My brother-in-law used to feel sorry for me and drop off groceries at our front door.

I had to apply for medical services and high-deductible health insurance. It took about a year before I sold my first article to a magazine called *Laptop*. I became "the router guy" in those early years, reviewing Wi-Fi devices and happily cashing the checks at the end of the month. By 2003, I started writing frequently for Wired.com, then the *Chicago Tribune*. For two years straight, way back then, I started my day writing in a journal.

During that season of life, trying to figure out how to stay productive with my time, I kept writing down my biggest challenges for the day, upcoming stresses, and overarching goals. By writing in a journal—usually over coffee—I set the tone for productivity for the entire day. I calibrated my thoughts, circled the challenges, crossed out any stressors, and reviewed my ambitions. It worked. I'd come up with a routine that became a habit.

Well over twenty years later, I'm still using the same basic routine.

Why Start Journaling?

In their 2013 bestselling book, *The ONE Thing: The Surprisingly Simple Truth Behind Extraordinary Results*, authors Gary Keller and Jay Papasan mention a curious stat about journaling. It turns out when we write down our goals and aspirations, we are 39.5 percent more likely to achieve them.[1] They didn't explain the reason, but we can make an educated guess. It's because we like to make things official.

There's something about jotting down a note that lodges that notation in our brains. Keller and Papasan go a step further and explain how writing down a goal and then seeking accountability— say, by sending someone an email about it—means we are 77.6 percent more likely to achieve the goal.[2]

The authors make a valid point. Only a few things *really matter*. When we record them, we decide what's important and what we'll remember. When we let chaos reign and allow multiple priorities to exist and wage war with one another, we end up never achieving anything. The reason I began to keep a journal so long ago, and the reason I'm still journaling today, is that I want to record (and ponder) what's really important. I want to match my daily activities with my biggest ambitions in life.

There are many things in life that define our purpose. Sometimes, it's a boss. They hand us a job description when we take a new role, and every meeting thereafter is meant to orient us toward that purpose. *Are we measuring up to the standards of the job description? Are we doing the most important activities the company requires?*

When we buck the system and make up our own rules about what matters, rarely aligning our tasks with our ambitions, we end up in a place where we are free to make up our own definitions about our life and call the shots every day. It's called *the unemployment line.*

When we were kids, our parents defined our purpose and set our tasks for the day. Others keep dictating our schedules in college . . . and marriage and life in general. Sure, as we get older there are times when we think we have more freedom. But the constant distractions of life and the wonderful opportunities we have at work become a jumble of confusion, competition, and chaos.

As adults, we have an incredible amount of freedom—we can stop at DQ anytime we want and buy the triple decker sundae. But with that freedom, how many of us are perfect at setting goals each day and always doing the most important tasks? I know I'm a long way from that ideal. I stop at DQ on occasion, which is fine once in a while. I sometimes get frustrated when I'm whiling away the time without intention and not reaching my goals.

Good routines such as writing in a journal each morning help you assess what is important and weed out the lower priorities. You're defining meaning and purpose in your life one day at a time. You minimize the impact of external factors such as stress or a busy schedule that often define our priorities and learn to defend yourself against constant distraction.

Ask yourself, Are the tasks you're completing the ones you really want to complete? Do they match up with your calling? Do they add up to the person you intend to be, or are they defining you on their own?

Good Intentions

Good productivity starts with both prioritizing tasks and effectively pursuing them with intention. Once I started writing in a journal to record my challenges, stressors, and ambitions, the tasks for the day became part of a more complete picture, one I was creating and recalibrating.

Journaling helps you keep track of what is working and what is distracting you and causing derailment. It's more than just a way to keep things organized. It's a way to remind yourself that you have a mission in life and a purpose and that there's a way to achieve that purpose if you stay focused.

Writing in a journal each morning carves out at least a few minutes to compose yourself during a set period. Did you catch that? *Compose yourself*, which means *become who you were meant to be*.

All it takes is seven minutes. That's it!

Before we talk about the journaling routine and explain how it all works, we need to clarify one important factor: we think more clearly in the morning than at any other time period, according to science.

If we can carve out a few moments after we wake up to chronicle what's about to transpire for the day, then we'll be productive.

That's the best definition of *productivity* I can give you: being intentional about what you do and why you do it each day. You might not be a morning person, but the only way to define the *what* and the *why* is to do it before you do anything else. Plus, as you'll see, you're smarter in the morning.

2

You're Smarter in the Morning

THE YEAR IS 1762. A servant rushes up the stairs of an apartment. He arrives at the same time each morning on the nose. The instructions are abundantly clear: don't wake up his master until the proper time.[1]

The servant pauses at the door and looks at the time, then waits patiently. The clock on a wall ticks over, and he enters the room to perform his duty: "Wake up, kind sir!" he announces, tapping a few times on the bedpost and leaving a pot of hot water and tea.

The man looks up at his servant with a dull expression. He's not wearing his wig, so his face looks like a squashed egg and his hair is matted and disheveled. (The truth is he always looks that way.)

The servant backs away, lowers his head, and closes the door. The online *Encyclopedia of Philosophy* describes the sleeping man as "quirky and dour"—he's a bit of an odd duck, that's for sure.

Sitting alone in a dark room, he finally reaches for his pipe. He's quiet and meditative, in a dull trance. He puffs for a few minutes and decides to pour himself a cup of black tea. It's always the same brand, and it's never too thick. The caffeine would not be enough to energize a mouse, but he still feels invigorated. It's not quite 5:30 a.m., but he has already pondered the upcoming events of the day:

Morning lecture
Lunch at the pub
Long walk
Go to bed

Still sitting in a dark room, he reaches for his books and papers. Then he lights a candle and scribbles notes for his class at the University of Königsberg in Prussia (present-day Poland and Russia).

At exactly 7:00 a.m. and not a moment sooner, he arrives at class. He explains how a depraved society must embrace morality. "From such crooked wood as that which man is made of, nothing straight can be fashioned," he says.[2] How depressing! Maybe he needed more tea. The man emotes about the ills of modern society and the law of order in government.

After class at exactly 11:00 a.m. each day, he leaves for lunch at the pub.

He eats one meal per day and never eats dinner. He lingers and chats with the patrons, who all know his name. By 3:30 p.m., he takes a long walk. It even has a name. It's now called *The Philosopher's Walk* and follows a leisurely route in the downtown area of Königsberg. It's always the same route and the same routine.*

* This story is somewhat fabricated from actual events. Think of it as one of those History Channel shows where people who are obviously California actors are playing the parts of Revolutionary War heroes. By the way, only twice in his life did Kant diverge from the predetermined path—once to buy a first edition copy of a philosopher friend's book (the masterwork by Jean-Jacques Rousseau about child education called *Emile*) and once to buy a newspaper announcing the French Revolution.

Why did he do it? The same routine each day: being awakened at the same time, smoking the same pipe, eating at the same pub. From 1762 until about 1802 (about forty years), his neighbors could set a clock on the wall at 3:30 p.m. when he started his daily walk.

You can imagine the conversation:

First bystander: There's that man with the egg-
                  shaped head!
Second bystander: Here, let me set the clock.

The man was Immanuel Kant, a philosopher who wrote some of the most important books about morality ever composed. The guy was extremely productive. One of the key reasons: he rose early in the morning and stuck to a daily routine. It never varied. While being that rigid is not the goal, Kant's routine does serve as an excellent starting point.*

∿∿∿

How does a morning routine help us? It locks us into a pattern, like eating breakfast at 7:00 a.m. every morning (that hopefully involves bacon). Because you can follow a routine without having to think too hard about the process, you develop patterns of thinking and habits that guide your actions.

Every good routine teaches you how to follow a habit that *sticks*.

Kant's routine is far too rigid and even a bit depressing. Lightening up on the tea and not having eggs every morning might have achieved the same results. But it shows that productive people stick to a schedule; they are intentional. Following a rou-

* Let me be clear: this story of Immanuel Kant shows the man was overly rigid about his schedule, and I'm not recommending that. We would call it OCD these days. At the same time, *routines do work*.

tine doesn't make you Adrian from the TV show *Monk*. It does mean you are more interested in following a repeatable routine than reinventing one each day.

Kant is in good company. Jeff Bezos likes to putter around the house for a few hours in the morning while the rest of us are stuck in commuter traffic.* The famous founder of Amazon wakes up and reads the same newspapers each day (including the one he owns, *The Washington Post*). He always pours a cup of coffee. Even though he's the richest person in the world, he probably burns the toast once in a while (or a staff member does), like most of us are prone to do. While he might not be as distracted by a monthly mortgage or a car that needs repairs, he does run a company with over eight hundred thousand employees.[3] Somehow, he doesn't seem stressed.

Unlike Kant, Bezos is not as rigid in the early morning hours. Instead, his workday doesn't start until 10:00 a.m. Yet he's extremely purposeful about mornings, knowing it's the period when we're more productive and even smarter. "I like to do my high-IQ meetings before lunch," he said in an interview with David Rubenstein in 2018. Because "by 5:00 p.m., I'm like 'I can't think about this today.'"[4]

What's going on here? Why was Immanuel Kant so overly habitual? Why does Bezos always do morning meetings? The reason is that a routine helps you start the day with predictable activities. Following a routine in the morning is a bit like swinging a golf club when you've been playing for decades. You do the same thing each morning so you can focus.

〰〰〰

In his book *What's Best Next: How the Gospel Transforms the Way You Get Things Done*, author Matt Perman describes how

---

* I drive a Toyota Camry. I am guessing Bezos lets someone else drive him around.

George Washington woke up each morning at 5:00 a.m. and started the day by giving orders to his staff. (I'll be honest and say I used to do the same thing with my kids.) The first president of the United States would eat a full breakfast at exactly 7:00 a.m., then ride around on his horse for about six hours.[5] That must have been a tough life, apart from the constant war conflicts.

Let's stop for a moment and ponder this. Immanuel Kant woke up at the same time each day, not using an alarm clock but relying on a worried servant. He wrote some of the most famous philosophical discourses in history before lunch. Jeff Bezos doesn't like to do anything that requires higher brainpower after lunch and prefers "focus time" over breakfast. George Washington followed the same routine each morning.

A smart approach for arguably the most brilliant philosopher in recent history, the richest person in the world, and the most famous founding father might also be a good approach for us, right? A morning routine works wonders. Surprise! It's also based on science.

∿∿∿

Your brain is more like a smartphone than you might want to admit. As humans, we charge up all night. When we wake up, we're ready to tackle more complex subjects, such as Kant describing morality to a depraved society or Amazon shipping products to people all over the world.

Experts say most of us are larks (alert in the morning) and some of us are owls (more lively at night). The owls are a curious bunch. Fantasy author Neil Gaiman used to compose most of his novels starting around 9:00 p.m. and working all night long.[6] The president of Southern Seminary, Albert Mohler, likes to start working at 11:00 p.m.[7] I once had a coworker at a startup in Minneapolis who worked from midnight until 10:00 a.m. each morning. The vast majority of us, however, are wired for clear thinking right after sunrise.

We're sharp as a tack then! Our brains are wired to focus intently first thing in the morning. According to author and professor Lisa Feldman Barrett, that's because a chemical in our brains called *norepinephrine* is in higher abundance when we wake up. While it might be hard to pronounce *norepinephrine*—especially in the morning without coffee—it's flowing freely.[8] The question is, How can we make the most of it?

When I wake up each morning, the words percolate before I ever touch a keyboard and work on an article. I sometimes come up with article ideas and even the opening lines of a column in the shower. It annoys everyone in my family, but I can't help it. It might explain why there are times when I can't remember if I've used the shampoo yet.

Like a coffee machine that drips hot water over ground-up coffee, my brain is mulling over what to write. Later in the day, my thoughts don't percolate in the same way. They feel more like a thick sludge.

Barrett told me why that's normal.[9] A gene clock fires up the norepinephrine right away in the morning (for most of us). We might call it the genetic version of Alexa or a timer on our smartphones. It's curiously complex, mostly because we are curiously complex humans. No one has ever been able to explain why norepinephrine even exists.

Being a morning person, she said, is based partly on the chemicals in your body and your metabolism, but it's also dictated by how you were raised, your background and experiences as a young adult, and your preferences as far as food and exercise (good choices or bad). Surprisingly, it's not the sugar in your cereal. Your metabolism is like a blueprint, designed to provide the clearest thought processes in the morning, not in the afternoon or at night.

Think of writing in a journal each morning as your *prime time*. You're *priming the pump* of insight. In this case, the pump is your brain. Our brains use one-fifth of our energy but are only one-fiftieth of our body mass.[10] Here's the crazy part. Barrett told me people are one standard deviation smarter in the morning. A standard deviation is about 15 points, so someone with a 115-point IQ will drop gradually to only 100 points later in the day. It explains why we watch so many sitcoms at night.

Since you're smarter in the morning, that's the best time to record your thoughts and make a list of challenges and ambitions.

If you're not a morning person and norepinephrine is most prevalent in the afternoon or evening, that's okay. I still recommend trying this routine in the morning before you start work or proceed with tasks. You'll find you're more perceptive, insightful, and consistent throughout the day even if you're not a morning person because you're still calibrating your thoughts. Not making a huge list, as I'll explain, and not goal setting yet—merely recording thoughts.

The main takeaway here? Be more like Kant. Model what Bezos does. Start fresh and record your insights. Write in a journal using the seven-minute routine in the morning. Your brain will thank you.

3

Capture the Hope Moments

AS THE DAY STARTS, hope has a mortal enemy. It's called *reality*. As productivity expert and author Nir Eyal once told me by phone, we have more hope in the morning.[1] Eventually the cold hard truth settles in.

Imagine this conversation:

Hope: Hello, world, it's going to be a wonderful day!

Reality: Dude, you really need to watch the news.

Hope: Why would I do that? I'm in a good mood, the sun is shining, and I just ate a full plate of scrambled eggs! Life is good!

Reality: Recent studies show that eggs are bad for you.

Hope: That's ridiculous! I'm personal friends with a few chickens! After all, I'm the one who makes the rooster crow in the morning! Chickens don't seem to have a care in the world, and that's all because of me!

Reality: You do know what happens to chickens eventually, don't you?

Hope: Hmm, they don't call it Kentucky Petting Zoo
Chicken, I guess.

Maybe you're a whiz at maintaining a high level of hope. My wife seems to keep hope alive all day and is also a big fan of exclamation marks.

Anyway! Most of us start out with brilliant ideas, new insights, and a wonderful outlook. It's possible to maintain that attitude all day, though most of us are quicker to accept reality. One key is to focus on what I call *hope moments*. They are a central theme in this book. In addition to writing down challenges and insights and recording any stressors, as I'll explain in the morning routine later, noting hope moments helps us uncover possibilities.

Hope moments occur in the morning before we watch the news and before we read any studies about how eggs, coffee, and butter on our toast are bad for us. It's also before we read other studies that eggs, coffee, and butter on our toast are all good for us. We write down hope moments so that we remember them.

Starting the Day with Hope

Why capture hope moments? For the morning routine, it's important to mull over the joys and sorrows of life, to write down the stressors, and to calibrate our life ambitions. Yet we mostly need hope.

You could argue that hope is the opposite of a goal. Hope is what *could be*; a goal is what *must be*. Hope has no limits; a goal is something confined and specific that must be tracked. I'm not against goals. It's just that hope should take precedence over goals and should drive us.

Think of hope moments as those small, delightful insights in the morning that come from somewhere beyond ourselves. There are no goals or tasks involved. Hope fills us with drive and passion whereas a goal is a limited and short-term undertaking;

it has a shelf life. Hope can help us overcome incredible suffering and disappointment; it can lead to a new career or help us find a spouse later in life. A goal gives us an objective to finish a marketing report by dinner. That's not too fulfilling.

A hope moment might be *maybe I will marry someone special.* The rush of expectation and the wonder of possibility set in! Where does the hope moment to get married someday rank on the productivity scale? Pretty high, I'd say. It's an aspiration worth recording in a journal for posterity, for sure. I've had hope moments like *maybe I will finish up an entire chapter of this book today* or *maybe I will figure out if I should move to another state.*

The concept of hope moments is brand-new and likely not something you have read about before because I invented the idea for this book. Recording them helps you connect the dots between *what you do today* and *your purpose in life.* This morning, I had a hope moment regarding someone calling me back about a new job opportunity. It's not wishful thinking. It's more like a spark or a light bulb, filling you with hope because it's based on real events, actual pursuits, and realistic expectations.

By recording hope moments, you're making sure you're aware of the patterns and connections in your life that lead to fulfillment. The word *fulfillment* means the achievement of something desired. Not knowing where you are going, what you are doing, or why you are doing it is the opposite of fulfillment. It leads to burnout, distracted living, and hopelessness.

∿∿∿

Sometimes, big ambitions seem unattainable. Author Charles Duhigg notes how it's important to step aside from our goals occasionally so that we can evaluate our bigger ambitions and decide if they are really worth attaining.[2] The morning routine is not meant for mere goal setting and task allocation. It's a way to ponder the day in an unstructured way. When we write down our ambitions and hopes in a journal, we're making a serious attempt to catalyze the ambitions we have into attainable, bite-sized nuggets that are far more achievable—life setting, not goal setting.

It worked for me. Early on, before my corporate career ended, I dreamed of becoming a full-time professional writer. I took small steps in that direction, but it wasn't until I started calibrating my aspirations and daily activities, making them sync up with my loftier ambitions, that I made any real progress. Long before I started writing, I recognized what was already bubbling up to the surface: that a corporate career was never the goal. I had other ambitions, and a daily morning journal helped me see that.

Calibrating Your Day

The morning routine helps you identify what's important before you do anything else. It's not the best time to plan out every detail of your day (see section 2 for that routine). For now, you're only jotting down and organizing your thoughts, avoiding too much actual planning. You're not deciding what to do for the day or picking tasks. You're not planning any projects, arranging meetings, or thinking ahead to lunch.

An early reader of this book who started the morning routine explained that the process puts a spring in his step: "Taking a few minutes out of my morning to be intentional about mindfulness made a big difference in my mood for the day. It allowed me to focus my energy on productivity and how I'm going to tackle my responsibilities and accomplish my goals later."

Think of the morning routine as something you do *before* goal setting. The morning routine helps you set more intentional goals later. It's a great way to fight against the deluge of information overload facing us daily.

When I do the routine, I jot down anything that comes to mind—concerns and fears, joys and sorrows. I don't make a task list; I make a John list. That sounds rather cliché, I know, but it's true. I rarely miss a day. On a recent camping trip to work on this book, my pen ran out of ink and I panicked. Then I realized I could do the morning routine on my phone.

This routine sets the tone for staying sharp and focused for the entire day. Once you jot down your initial thoughts to define what has the most meaning and purpose for you, you'll prime the pump of insight and record hope moments. You've put yourself on the path of productivity with purpose.

4

Put Yourself on the Right Path

SOME OF US MAKE PRODUCTIVITY an exercise in futility. We make it hard to get anything done. Imagine someone trying to avoid notifications on their phone and seeing text messages but who keeps their plastic gizmo close at hand all day. Or picture someone trying to lose weight who keeps candy at their desk.

The secret to good productivity is to put yourself on a path where it's easier to make decisions that are beneficial and efficient. If your phone constantly distracts you, it might be time to leave it in the car when you are working on a tough project. If you need to wash the dishes and prepare for guests coming over, cue up a kid's show or set a board game on the kitchen table to give the minions something to do.

Productivity is all about pathfinding. The morning routine is like taking out a map (remember those?) and deciding which path to take. It's like tying our shoes before stepping on an escalator.

As we grow and mature, our ability to be productive grows as well. If we're patient or kind, it's not because we suddenly decided to have those attributes. They developed over time and matured in us.

I believe good productivity is the same. We're efficient with our time not in a *single moment* for one project but all day long. We are efficient when we help our kids with homework or clean the garage not because we suddenly formulated a good work ethic on the spot. It's because we developed productivity-enhancing traits one day at a time, one project at a time, and one minute at a time. Sudden bursts of productivity never last anyway.

As you'll see, the morning routine helps with good decision-making. When you have the right mindset, you are prepared to face challenges, setbacks, and distractions. You are in the right headspace.

Making Good Decisions

Each decision you make either puts you on the path of good productivity with purpose or derails you and puts you on a path of inefficiency, not to mention depression and anxiety. But how do you know which decisions you need to make? The answer is to be selective about them and prepared.

In a podcast called *No Stupid Questions* from late 2020, author and researcher Angela Duckworth mentions how we often make the easiest decision but not the right decision.[1] We like to avoid conflict. My favorite author, Bill Bryson, has written about how humans are wired to eat as much food as we can because we don't know where we will find food next.[2] We make snap decisions; we don't put a lot of thought into them.

We are not on the right path. We're stumbling into poor productivity.

Here's the rub: we're all overworked. We might as well figure out how to become more efficient instead of constantly getting sidetracked and waylaid. The alternative is to battle against time and our own bad habits. This is where a little brain science can help once again.

^^^

The *executive function* in our brains involves the choices we make—right and wrong, good and bad, moral and immoral. Executive function takes place in the frontal lobe. That part of the brain helps us determine if something is true. For example, as a journalist, I'm often asked by readers how I can tell whether a statement is true and how I verify sources. They are hinting at fake news and how to know if something is accurate, whether it's on CNN or Fox News. For me, it means using the executive function to analyze the facts. I tell them it involves laborious decisions.

And every decision matters. You could say that your entire life is a culmination of small decisions. Small, good decisions lead to joy and fulfillment. Bad decisions lead to a life of regret and hopelessness.

Recording your thoughts each day makes you more aware of where your decisions are leading you. Is the path one that helps or hinders? Are you more aware of what you are doing, how you are doing it, and why?

Another well-known section of the brain is the *amygdala*. This is where things get interesting. The amygdala controls emotion and stress. It comes into play when you drive in heavy traffic, someone swerves in front of you, and you raise a fist in anger. Or you go out on a date as a teenager and think you have found Mr. Right but discover he is oh so wrong for you. (A quick side note: the concept of *stress* is relatively new. In 1947, endocrinologist Hans Selye first studied how hormones in mice respond to stimulus and called it stress.[3]) When I'm stressed and then discover donuts in the house, I'll be more likely to eat them. Thanks, amygdala!

So we make executive-function decisions in the frontal lobe. We make emotional decisions in the amygdala. One handles practical decisions, and one handles emotional decisions.

Here's the good news: we have full control over both!

Each day, you have the ability to resist bad decisions. You have the ability to resist an emotional response. It's this calculus that matters. When you do the morning routine, it's your chance to put yourself on the right path. You're like a windup toy that runs fast, efficiently, and smoothly.

Being on the right path means we're not overloaded with stress and decision-fatigue, so we're in a state where good decisions are likely.

Choose Joy

After leaving my corporate job in 2001, I struggled to find my footing in the work world. No health insurance at the time, no regular paycheck.

I often felt exhausted and discouraged, and the stress of this constant instability and insecurity in life was waging a war inside of me. It was winning, and I was not on a good path. I'd come home from a business trip or after working on projects with little success, and I'd fall in a slump on the sofa. I'd watch whatever show was on television at the time.

Professor and author Jordan Peterson has often described how stress and depression work in his classroom lectures. This was before he became famous for his book *12 Rules for Life: An Antidote for Chaos*. It involves several layers. We are dealing with stressors at work . . . and then we add sickness. Our kids are not doing well at school . . . and we back up into another car at the grocery store. He describes how we have a weak point, and then something breaks—the foundation gives out. Imagine a chair with four legs. One of the legs is a bit wobbly (marriage trouble). Add more stress on top of the chair (job loss) with a leg that's weak and ready to break, and *crash*.[4]

Joy is a decision we have to make. We choose joy or we choose sorrow. What path will we choose? How will we start the day? Will it be with joy?

One night, I assembled the ducklings. My four kids were barely in elementary school; my youngest daughter was only three. I remember where I was sitting and how I was recalling a Bible verse from the morning.

I decided right then to choose joy.

We held a wrestling match in the living room, and the shouts of joy were loud and clear. I'm not exactly petite—I'm six feet, two inches tall and, at the time, weighed 220 pounds. I'm Scandinavian. My ancestors probably plundered neighboring towns. I towered over my kids, but I cowered on the ground instead like a weakling and let them pin me.

One, two, three . . . out for the count. They all took turns.

What happened next is quite revealing. Joy filled me up. I was remarkably productive the next day, and then the next.

In 2002, the words started flowing, and they never stopped.

I wrote with a clear mind and a clear purpose. My fingers tapped with joy and my thoughts flowed like butter. To this day, I can't quite explain my boundless productivity. This book is at least an attempt to account for what has worked, even if the truth of that joyful overflow these last twenty years is mostly due to a blessing from God. Not every day has put me on the path of productivity, joy, stillness, and hope . . . but most days have.

I've been joyfully writing now for so long I sometimes forget where it all started. In that living room, wrestling with my kids.

Neuroscientists have been saying for years there's a reason we think more negative thoughts than positive thoughts. They blame cortisol, the fight-or-flight hormone that often dictates how we make snap decisions.[5]

Cortisol flows more freely in our brain. It's related to feelings of stress and anxiety, and we seem to be wired to experience it. Scientists say this wiring is related to our fight-or-flight mechanism. Dopamine, which is a chemical in our brains related to the reward system, doesn't flow as freely as cortisol.

The next time you have a negative thought, remember: it came easier.

What's the solution? In a popular article for Inc.com in 2019, I wrote about the bounce principle.[6] I learned it from a friend many years ago. A quick summary: when you have a negative thought, bounce it away, wrestle with your kids, set aside work conflicts, and find strength in joy.

Put yourself on the path. Learn to recognize how the choices you make either help you stay productive or cause soul-crushing defeat. The difference? It has to do with how you start your day each morning.

Seven-Minute Morning
ROUTINE

The seven-minute morning routine is where it all starts. To understand more about any of these steps, be sure to reread the previous chapters above, which explain why this routine is so valuable for productivity.

▶ **BEFORE YOU START:** *Prepare*

Find a quiet place that's far away from distractions. Power down your phone and stash it away. Clear a spot for journaling and for your coffee cup (if you have one). You might have to find a corner of the office. Make sure you have a nice journal. Choose a high-quality pen that will make journaling effortless and fun. Use a watch or a kitchen timer and set it for a seven-minute countdown.

▶ **MINUTE ONE:** *Clear Your Head*

Clearing your head is the first step of the seven-minute morning routine. For sixty seconds, think about what your day will entail, but don't write anything down, and don't start making a task list. Just think. What are the challenges facing you? Why do they matter? Get ready to dive into the routine with gusto and with intentional effort. Your timer should be counting down the first minute as you prepare your thoughts.

▶ **MINUTE TWO:** *Breathe a Little*

You have an idea of what is facing you today. You have thought about the day and what might be coming up. Great! Now spend another sixty seconds (counting down to minute five on your timer) and breathe in and out. Take deep breaths in and exhale in an exaggerated way. You are not starting the day with overload; you are starting out with focus and intention. If you get bored doing the breathing, that's okay. We all do. Sit back and relax, take a sip of coffee, look out the window. You're preparing your mind.

▶ MINUTES THREE THROUGH SIX: *Write Notes*

Now it's time to get down to business. You may have noticed this routine is highly regimented. You have exactly four minutes to write down some light notes. You're not planning your day (that's the plan your day routine). Write down a few random thoughts about the day. Don't make a task list! Write down some things you are looking forward to plus a few stressors and challenges. During this time, also record hope moments. These are the insights that came to you when you first woke up, had a devotional time, or sat and pondered what was coming up today earlier in this routine.

▶ MINUTE SEVEN: *Debrief*

When the timer hits minute one in the countdown, it means you are almost done! Now go back and review your notes and circle the most pressing concern. Cross off any stressors. Also be sure to circle a hope moment. That's it! You completed the seven-minute morning routine.

Plan Your Day

The things that are the most important
do not always scream the loudest.

—BOB HAWKE, FORMER
AUSTRALIAN PRIME MINISTER

5

Learn How to Focus

BEFORE WE DIVE INTO PLANNING your day more effectively, let's cover all the things competing for your attention. Or at least—the one thing.

It's a shiny, little handheld gadget.

As author John Mark Comer notes, young adults know the drill. He mentions how 77 percent of young adults surveyed said that when nothing else is capturing their attention, they reach for their phones.[1]

Comer does an excellent job explaining the white noise that's all around us, the constant pings, chirps, and chimes. While writing this book, I noticed the McDonald's app changed their notification sound. It's now the familiar tune they play in their commercials: "Dada da da da." Sorry for getting it stuck in your head if you know it, but that's the point, right? There's only one goal, and it's to make sure you buy more hamburgers.

According to a study conducted by Cornell University, we make about thirty-five thousand decisions per day.[2] I have a theory about how we make so many. One of my journal entries recently shed some light on it. I had written down the phrase

50-millisecond rule.[3] I didn't understand why it was there until recently. (Apparently, I was telling myself to spend a little more than fifty milliseconds researching that rule.) It comes from the world of web design. It means when someone visits a website, they take about fifty milliseconds to decide if the visual presentation is worth their time.

The same rule applies to all our decisions: which apps to install and keep on our phones, which people to date, which burgers to buy, and so on. We are inundated with decisions all day long. There are a million priorities.

In biblical times, putting on "a yoke" implied a way of thinking and being. Jesus said his yoke was easy and light (Matthew 11:29–30 NIV). He was suggesting a way of thinking and making decisions that was not all about the pings and chimes of life but rather about finding purpose. Productivity guru Stephen Covey wrote frequently that planning your day is mostly about aligning your tasks and daily schedule with the things you care about most.[4] (If you're keeping track, you're correct: I just mentioned Jesus and Stephen Covey in the same paragraph.)

So before planning your day, first put on the yoke, which limits distractions and sidetracks. This helps. You still have decisions to make once you narrow things down. As economist Thomas Sowell says, "Life does not ask what we want. It presents us with options."[5] All we have to do is select them.

Where You Focus Becomes Your Greatest Area of Success

In 2016, I wrote an article for my Inc.com column called "Where You Focus Will Become Your Greatest Area of Success."[6] Readers emailed me to say it helped them make tough decisions in their jobs. In the article, I explained how my focus on writing led to amazing success—for example, millions of readers. I didn't try to become a public speaker at the same time. I wasn't simultaneously taking scuba diving lessons. I focused on writing and, for ten years, mostly wrote the Inc.com columns I posted once per day.

At the time, I wasn't aware of the fact that brain scientists had already made a similar finding—that multitasking doesn't work.

"Emphasis is more important than effort," I wrote in the column. "Effort is a push, a drive—it's the hours in a day. It means you are spending a lot of energy on something. Yet, you can spend a lot of time and put a lot of effort into a project and still discover you've failed because you lack emphasis. For emphasis, you have to stop doing everything else."

Many books on productivity say roughly the same thing— that you must set *parameters*. Author and speaker Nir Eyal calls it *timeboxing*; author and professor Adam Grant uses the term *time blocking*. (More on these in chapter 6.)

By following the seven-minute routines in this book, you make sure that you focus for short periods. The result is you form a new habit over time. You're teaching yourself what these experts call *implementation intentions*. Adam Grant uses a time block to work on a research paper for four hours; in this book, I'm asking for only seven minutes.*

∧∧∧

In his bestseller *The Obstacle Is the Way*, marketing expert Ryan Holiday notes that passing along self-help advice or trumpeting a formula for success isn't his goal. He doesn't want to provide all the answers. He is going for something much deeper: finding purpose in life.[7]

Experts such as Nir Eyal, James Clear, and many others ask us to search within ourselves as we struggle to find meaning in life.

---

* The routines teach you *the habit of focus*. The timed structure, the specific items to write down or track, and the entire process are designed to set parameters on your time. The result is that you learn to set parameters on other tasks too, such as writing a business report. The routines are also about as easy and accessible as learning how to start a car.

They also emphasize purpose but tend to present theories and ideas that can help us improve from a naturalistic or humanist perspective. If we dig deep enough and try hard enough and struggle long enough, we'll eventually become a better version of ourselves.

I want to go a few steps further. After all, I believe purpose is external to us. Our purpose isn't merely to improve as humans and nothing else. To the naturalist, self-improvement is always the ultimate goal. To me, we improve in order to help others or to free up more of our time for things that matter.

One of my most wonderful discoveries as an adult—as a husband and a father who has raised my kids and who is now in my second act as a book author—is to realize that purpose is not something we find within ourselves by soul-searching. As humans, we're made for bigger things.

Good productivity, in a similar way, is a pursuit of the external. You could say there is no such thing as self-improvement. We grow and become more efficient not because we're selfish and want to become better at life. We improve because we want to serve, help others, and make a difference. It's who we are; we're created to work hard because we have purpose.

This perspective frees us up to see productivity differently. It relieves the pressure. We don't have to improve because we care only about our stuff. We improve because it helps the world. We become aware of how temporal life is. We yearn to make the most of our time because time is a precious commodity.

The goal is always to stop and think about whether we are using the time we have wisely. "I would have written a shorter letter, but I did not have the time," said the mathematician Blaise Pascal.[8] It's a statement for our age. When we use time wisely, we are more intentional and purposeful.

~~~

One step in the planning routine involves *removing* tasks. An early reader for this book told me she has an extremely hard time doing that. We like to have long lists of things to do because that makes us feel productive and valuable. However, as author Laura Vanderkam notes, we sometimes need to say no to things to free up the extra space we need.

The extra space helps us think of new ideas and formulate plans. The free time helps us become the person we want to be. "Sometimes being a little less responsive allows you the space to come up with the ideas that make people want to work with you in the first place," Vanderkam writes.

Vanderkam also advocates for a "later" list. When you think of something you need to do, write it down but don't necessarily make a plan to complete that task, she says. A later list is just that: things to do later. She calls these juicy little "productive distractions" valuable and important, but they can also derail what you really intended to do for the day.[9] As author Jordan Raynor told me by Zoom chat, completing everything won't create purpose.[10]

How to Be Decisive about Decisions

Stress will come eventually. It always does. Some of our choices during the day will be under duress. We need to learn how to become more decisive beforehand. As philosopher William James warned, "There is no more miserable human being than one in whom nothing is habitual but indecision, and for whom the lighting of every cigar, the drinking of every cup, the time of rising and going to bed every day, and the beginning of every bit of work are subjects of express volitional deliberation."[11]

As Ryan Holiday explains, "Good decisions are not made by those who are running on empty."[12] We define for ourselves what is important and let the day unfold accordingly. When we plan the day, we remove the pressure of performance. We are free to make mistakes without thinking personal success is the ultimate reward.

At the end of his book *Stillness Is the Key*, Holiday touches on a key concept you will find throughout this book: it's okay to rest and be intentional with our time. There's no rush. He explains how he once stared down a bull in his yard. He had to move slowly and deliberately, planning every step. The goal was not to stir up trouble with the bull or to create havoc. (The bull ended up crashing through a nearby fence.)[13]

Planning your day is similar to facing down a bull.

We have to be deliberate.

We can't let old habits rise to the surface and rule the day.

We have to *plan for patience*.

By focusing on one thing at a time and one meeting at a time and also on how we plan to have that type of focus, we avoid the temptation to try to rush through problems or resolve them quickly. Maybe the bull we're facing is a two-year-old in a tirade or Microsoft Excel. Whatever it is, the idea is to ruthlessly eliminate distraction by deliberate and intentional focus.

What comes next? Get ready for a chapter on why you should stop relying on lists. A word of caution before proceeding: list people might not like it.

6

Stop Relying So Much on Lists

Rahul Vohra is one of the smartest guys you'll ever meet. *GQ* once described him as "a slender English gentleman of Indian extraction who's 50% hair and 50% brain."[1] When he talks, he sounds a bit like he went to Cambridge (because he did) and yet he faces the same challenges we all do. He's overloaded with meetings, has a bulging inbox, and can't set priorities perfectly. Taming our inboxes is a universal struggle (he started a company called Superhuman that makes it easier to manage your email), and we'll address it in part two of this book when we discuss bad habits. However, Vohra is also a precise and intentional person. Here's just one example.

To manage his schedule, he uses a timeboxing method that might surprise you. Timeboxing is a well-known productivity strategy. It means you stack your meetings and your tasks to become more efficient. I've been doing this for many years but didn't have the name for it until recently. I wanted to be productive, so I grouped all my interviews on Monday afternoon one after the other. Sometimes, I had to negotiate with people to accommodate my grouped-interview plan (it didn't always work).

I also timeboxed my tasks. With this book, I did long research sessions, then I made revisions to the manuscript. I avoided frequently switching back and forth between tasks. This timeboxing method is central to the planning routine in this book.

Timeboxing is brilliant because it means you don't lose momentum or focus during that time period. You're on a roll. Vohra holds all his one-on-one meetings with direct reports on Tuesdays. He assigns priorities to them and notices how these priorities flow through the company during the week. "Sometimes a problem is solved by Friday that we discussed in one of those Tuesday meetings," he says.[2]

Vohra takes timeboxing to another level though. Instead of inbox zero for email he calls it *Calendar 100%*. The goal is to account for his time as accurately as possible. His day is jam-packed. He meets with investors; he holds team meetings. On the collaborative messaging app Slack, he types a message to his assistant when he switches tasks. He might decide to work on a new business proposal for an investor for an hour, then switch to another task to plan a team outing for thirty minutes. At the end of each day, his assistant sends him a report on how he spent his time and then his assistant creates a schedule that relies on timeboxing to improve his day.

That might seem like Vohra is taking things too far. But he says it's important because he's building a brand-new product. (Maybe he will loosen up a bit once the company becomes more well-known.)

Vohra doesn't ever stress out about his schedule. "If I discover I only spent about 30 percent of my time during the week on recruiting, I make adjustments," he says. "I have more agency to do the things that matter most."

Curiously, he doesn't rely too much on lists. He does create a schedule and plan his day based on timeboxing and feedback from his assistant, and the seven-minute planning routine you'll read about later in this section is designed to help you do the same thing. It's one reason his Superhuman email app doesn't show a list of messages. It shows them one at a time. When you browse emails you see one full page for each message. You use the arrow key to see the next email.

It's brilliant. No lists, just one email at a time.

You might be a bit "list happy" and are having trouble imagining what life would be like without them. I feel your pain. Full disclosure: I also like lists. I make a list of camping supplies for trips. I make a grocery list. An early reader of this book told me she would be lost without lists. She said, "When I read the title of this chapter, I got offended . . . haha! I love making lists—they rule my day at work and at home, otherwise I forget things. I also love checking off things on my to-do list."

Maybe you can relate.

The problem is that lists create a cognitive load on our brains. It's better to focus on where we'll spend our time—which topics we'll address, who will be at meetings, how we'll prioritize our day—and avoid constantly making task lists for everything in life just because we can or because that's what seems to work the best. With apologies to the countless task list apps out there, a task list is a secondary tool. It's more important to manage our time than our tasks, as we'll see. It's more important to have a plan and set top priorities than to canonize everything.

Your Time Is Everything

One reason the seven-minute plan your day routine works so well is that, as humans, we're constantly trying to predict outcomes. What's our role at the meeting later in the day? Will we impress the boss? Do we need to book a plane ticket to Miami? How much will it cost? This constant prediction tendency is based on very recent discoveries in neuroscience about how we process information and look to the future. One finding is related to how dopamine works in our brains.

You might think dopamine is part of a reward system for what you are experiencing *right now*. With that feeling of euphoria when you eat an ice-cream cone, you would think the dopamine arrives after you take your first bite. Scientists now know the dopamine arrives long before you visit Dairy Queen.[3] It arrives when you plan to make the visit—more accurately, it's *when you decide to buy the ice cream*. The reward kicks in at that moment, predicting a future outcome.

We're always living in the future. It's one reason disappointment feels so terrible. We already made the plan, we already experienced the reward, and then—no ice cream.

As humans, we prefer predictability. In studies about how people deal with stress, the results are not surprising—we tend to pick the outcome that will involve the least amount of effort and the least amount of anxiety. While we don't need a scientific study to tell us a lack of control over the outcome makes us anxious, it sure helps to know that's exactly what scientists found out. It's also obvious to anyone who has taken an exam, gone on a blind date, or visited the dentist.

A task list doesn't work because it doesn't help us focus on what's important. It just helps us complete the list. A better way to plan is to *resist the list*. Draw a line through tasks. Group (or timebox) your meetings. It's always better to prioritize a few items than to make a list of everything we need to do and then mindlessly complete even the secondary tasks.

∧∧∧

Our brains are constantly trying to predict sensory inputs and judge whether something is worth the effort. It's not like I'm saying we can control the neurons in our brains with exact precision, but I am suggesting that the regimen to plan our day will alleviate some of the stress about outcomes and the need to complete tasks and constantly maintain a list.

When we set parameters for the day, we predict outcomes. It's not the laundry list that matters. It's which laundry to do and when and why today is even the right day to wash clothes. It's a deeper exercise.

As it turns out, there are two modes of thinking involved when we make plans—*active mode* and *default mode*.[4] (I sometimes add a third option called *don't want to think about anything mode*.) With active-mode thinking, we're more precise and detailed. Active-mode thinking is what you'll use during the seven-minute routine to plan your day. It's meant to help you formulate plans and develop better habits. When you do that, there's some good news. You are giving yourself more flexibility and latitude for the second type of thinking. With default-mode thinking, you'll free yourself to daydream and brainstorm more effectively. One summary of how human beings exist in the world could be this: we do our active-mode (details) thinking so that we gain more time for default-mode (free-form) thinking.

Let's review. Making a task list is tempting because then we feel as if we accomplished something. But active thinking and planning with the daily routine means we address all the variables, including what we will do with our time, why we are doing the tasks, and how we will do them.

What Works Better than Lists

What's the secret to dealing with cognitive load on our brains? Of having too many things on our lists and not making progress?

Productivity gurus such as James Clear, Charles Duhigg, and many others talk about making small changes in our routines. In his book *Atomic Habits*, for example, James Clear mentions how doing one push-up per day is much better than setting a goal to do ten or twenty.[5] Why is that? Because it's a small step in the right direction and helps us form the habit. First comes the routine (doing one push-up in the morning), then comes the habit (becoming the type of person who does push-ups every morning).

A routine to plan your day helps you start small. You'll expand from there, but the goal is to become someone who is a daily planner as opposed to someone who buys a daily planner and lets it sit on a shelf week after week. When something is a habit, it becomes second nature. It's far better to be a daily planner than to merely own one or say you use one. It is much better to become someone who completes your work than someone who makes lists about work.

It's okay to list out a few items in the planning routine. What I'm really suggesting, however, is that constantly writing down a long list of priorities is the very thing that hampers productivity at times. You are doing *everything*. The question is whether you are doing the *right* things.

Shorter Lists, Better Results

A quick summary so far: long lists don't really work. Instead, planning your day by choosing priorities helps relieve cognitive load. You'll mull over the important tasks only. As you write in your journal, you define the meaning and purpose that matter most to you. This winnowing helps you compare the tasks of the day with your overall goals and ambitions. The plan your day routine might involve doing less but focusing more.

The routines all help you develop healthy habits. You'll avoid decision fatigue and "analysis paralysis" when it comes to knowing what is important, as opposed to making sudden and random decisions in the moment or all day long. You will know what should be an a priori task. As an example, my son-in-law makes two short lists, one for the week and one for each day. Sometimes, that daily list has only one item on it.

You'll be tested during the day, of course. A good routine in the morning such as writing in a journal or planning your day sets a pattern. Later, you might be faced with decisions that go against who you want to become.

Failure is part of life. It takes sixty-six days to develop good habits according to scientific studies, and those estimates are based on actual neuroscience related to how long it takes to develop new neural pathways.[6] You should expect some setbacks. As entrepreneur Arianna Huffington has said, failure is part of success. It's not the opposite of success.[7]

We all form new habits whether we intend to or not. The question is, Which habits will we form? Good ones or bad ones? Once we recognize the need to form a habit, we may not attain it right away. As Charles Duhigg notes, change is hard. What pushes us along is often a new idea, a success story, an example of what works, or an external inspiration. Often, accountability with other people helps us succeed.[8]

Several years ago, a friend of mine became the inspiration for me to lose weight. He started biking, walking, and hiking almost every day, and he made good food choices. We met for breakfast at least once a week. I had eggs and toast. He ate granola.

One of us became thinner. He started shrinking one week at a time.

I asked him recently why he developed those new habits and acknowledged how he was an example for my own life. I mentioned he seemed to be making changes for health reasons. He said it wasn't out of a fear of poor health but a fear of not living life to the fullest. He wasn't worried about his health; he wanted more out of life.

Since losing weight myself, I've noticed I fit much more comfortably in a kayak and on a bike. I can do things that were not possible before. James Clear calls these *non-scale victories*.[9] I wasn't measuring my weight loss by the scale but rather by what the dieting helped me achieve.

Duhigg labels the initial, seemingly minor shifts in what we do and how we approach life the *keystone habits*.[10] For me, it was choosing the granola. Then it became the realization that I could fit in a kayak.

As William James, the philosopher and psychologist who lived in the late 1800s, stated, "Do a thing with difficulty the first time, but soon do it more and more easily, and finally, with sufficient practice, do it semi-mechanically, or with hardly any consciousness at all."[11]

Now that you're equipped with the permission to stop making such long lists and trying to do everything, and with the knowledge that the real goal is to work on the right tasks with more purpose, the next step is to figure out which tasks might be complex and challenging but potentially the most valuable.

7

Do the Most Important Tasks First

HERE ARE TWO of my favorite statistics: the average person lives on this planet for about 2,522,880,000 seconds and breathes about 672,768,000 times in a lifetime.[1] That's how much time we have if we live to the age of eighty. It's a lot, but it also seems remarkably precise. In the time it takes you to read this page you might breathe in and out about fifty times.

Time is of the essence. That's why I'm about to ask you to accomplish less, to prioritize your tasks, and even to label some of them a certain way.

I mentioned in the previous chapter that making lists doesn't really work. It increases the cognitive load on our brains; we finish our list because we like to finish *something*. What works better is planning our time and prioritizing tasks, and that process starts with picking the critical tasks.

This doesn't always mean choosing pertinent tasks. It does mean choosing meaningful tasks—that is, the ones that lead to the most benefit.

In case you are wondering, hard tasks are sometimes the most meaningful and provide the most benefit. Psychologist Edwin Locke did several studies back in 1968 to prove that once and for all. He showed how survey participants had a higher level of worth and accomplishment when they took on tasks that were harder and more challenging.[2] We like to convince ourselves that easy and urgent tasks should be accomplished first. Then we like to make lists of all those easy urgent tasks. Planning your day will require a much deeper calibration.

Finding the Truth in Your Priorities

Focus is hard. It requires effort and a process to find success. One reason the seven-minute plan your day routine works so well is that we can determine which tasks are the most important. As Bullet Journal creator Ryder Carroll explained to me, writing things down and making plans is a way to prioritize what matters most.[3]

If you write something down and it's stressing you out, cross it off as you should be doing in the morning routine. (In his method, Carroll provides a notation that means *delete*.)

Curiously, the word *priorities* didn't exist before the 1400s. Only the singular word *priority* existed.[4] And before that, the older word *priori* meant "knowledge considered to be true without being based on previous experience or observation." There's a theme here. We keep changing the words to match the culture and our crazy schedules. Planning our day for seven minutes means we set the priori—we determine what is true and valid for that day and exclude lesser truths. Prioritization equals truth.

Why bother? According to recent research related to the modern office environment, workers are interrupted every eleven minutes.[5] The same researchers also found it can take about one-third of the day to recover from those constant interruptions. Obviously, this research was conducted long before COVID-19 and the current trend to let people work at home. I suspect the time needed to restart our work is even longer during a crisis.

Planning our day helps us collect our thoughts, similar to the morning routine. We are thinking machines, after all. There's a curious statistical discrepancy though. In 2012 when the book *The ONE Thing: The Surprisingly Simple Truth Behind Extraordinary Results* came out, the authors noted that humans have four thousand thoughts per day.[6] Recent research, especially using MRI scans, has estimated that a thoughtful person might have more like fifty to seventy thousand thoughts per day.[7]*

One estimate suggests we have a new thought every fourteen seconds![8] While this research is making a blanket statement about our curious minds, there are a few implications—namely, that we are easily distractible, jump from one thought to the next, and need to learn to have more focus.

Dr. David Meyer, a researcher at the University of Michigan who has conducted task-switching studies, estimates that constantly switching tasks is incredibly inefficient. It means we spend 25 percent more time working when we switch tasks.[9] Complex tasks, such as moving from writing a document to calculating a budget, can increase the time by as much as 100 percent.

Think about what that means for your daily work. If you have multiple priorities each day (e.g., you create a long list of things to do, which we discussed in the previous chapter) and attempt to complete them all, you are constantly running uphill. Let's say you have ten different tasks throughout the day. One is to create a marketing plan, one is to schedule some posts on social media, another is to write a blog, and so on. If you spread them all out, and each task takes you thirty minutes, you might think you'd spend about five hours total. Sadly, that's not the case.

* I tend to overthink just about everything, so maybe my numbers are higher. My wife would argue I can think about absolutely nothing at times, so maybe they are in the lower range.

Distractions, setbacks, and the lag and ramp-up time to start new tasks increases your time dramatically.

If it ever feels like you are not getting things done and you find yourself working late into the night, there's a reason. You are on a task treadmill.

It's why productivity experts harp about timeboxing, which groups tasks in a way that avoids disruption and keeps you in the flow of work. That's why the plan your day routine is so critical. We prioritize and plan, we account for breaks and downtime, we timebox, and we schedule our activities as a way to free up more time for the things that matter in life.

As an example, when you group similar tasks together (timeboxing), such as writing a blog and scheduling social media posts, you will expend less effort and experience a smoother flow of productivity.

I really want to stress at this point that the routine to plan your day is meant to be abundantly simple. It's not complex, and that's intentional. It's you and a journal or a piece of paper, choosing your priorities. There may be times when, like my son-in-law, you write down only one task. You'll spend time thinking about why that task is important and when to do it.*

The implications here are profound. Psychologist Wayne Oates first invented the term *workaholic* in 1947 as a variation of the word *alcoholic*—it was meant as a joke, but it's not.[10] The compulsion to drink dates back nine thousand years or more.[11] Long before that, humans fought many other vices. It seems we're hardwired to make bad decisions. Just when we think we've kicked one bad habit, we find another one.

When a new employee shows up at work, we don't have to train them to be a workaholic. It comes naturally to all of us. They dive into work like a teenager trying to find a date for prom—that is, with full conviction and without much planning. Workahol-

---

* My daughter once had a task list with one item. It read: get married today.

ism is now an admired trait. Yet recent studies have shown that someone who works more than eleven hours per day has a 67 percent higher chance of developing heart disease.[12] Constant overworking is also a major cause of depression and stress.[13]

Seth Godin, marketing guru and book author, has said some of us say yes to things that should have been a no.[14] The plan your day routine is partly (mostly?) a time to figure what should be a no. As Tom Friel, retired CEO of the executive search firm Heidrick & Struggles, has noted, it's important to be quick to say no to things that don't matter and slow to say yes to things that will require the most effort.[15]

How to Pick the Most Important Tasks

For many of us, our most pressing tasks fall into three distinct groups. The first group is what we'll call the *inside tasks*. These are the things you need to own; they belong to you and no one else. If you don't do the inside tasks, no one else will. Think of the sales manager who needs to assign phone calls to the staff. No one else can do that. If the sales manager doesn't plan those objectives, the company will suffer.

The second group involves *outside tasks*. You may already know what these are if you have worked in an office where people blame and shame you into doing their work for them. For example, you're a graphic artist but for some reason you find yourself scheduling social media posts. An outside task is something that impacts you and could fall into your lap but is not pertinent.

Many of these tasks swirling around in your head are not really your concern. They become pertinent to you because someone else isn't doing their job. Outside tasks are usually lower in priority than inside tasks. They could become part of your repertoire, especially if your boss asks you to do them, but for daily planning purposes, it's better to minimize your outside tasks.

The third group is the most troubling as far as working too much, multitasking too often, and burning up too many brain cells. These are the *never tasks*. In the modern office, a never task is something you should never do because it's outside of your job description. For some reason, you do them anyway. Often, these are the tasks that make up that long list you might be using each day and that might be destroying productivity.

We think about never tasks all day long, we ponder why they exist—we stress out over them. When you do the seven-minute routine to plan your day, you are free to cross the never tasks off your list.

A never task might be something obvious—such as sweeping out the break room (unless that's your job). In my job, a never task might involve editing. (Shout-out to the person editing this manuscript. You're awesome, thank you.) Sure, you might do never tasks to show you're a team player, but when you plan your day, leave these never tasks out. Don't think about them, don't add them to an app, and don't worry about them.

Never tasks often slink their way onto your task list because no one else wants to do them, or perhaps you are too nice to say no to them. Never tasks take much longer to complete because they are outside of your expertise and you likely lack the motivation to complete them.

As Ryder Carroll told me, these are also the tasks we do that lack purpose and meaning. We end up hating our jobs and burning out, even if we follow a good process to complete them and even if they are assigned to us.[16] "We are what we repeatedly do," wrote Will Durant, paraphrasing Aristotle.[17] When we repeatedly do never tasks, we become bored and unmotivated.

Of course, an inside task can become an outside task if your job changes or you're promoted. An outside task can change and evolve, becoming a never task. The point is to identify *for today* which tasks are yours alone, ancillary and loosely related to your job, or not at all your job. My hope is you cross more things off your list than you leave standing or add.

In the plan your day routine, you'll also make a note about your critical goals. I'll explain how those work in the next chapter.

Suffice it to say, we covered a lot. The basic summary is this: write down your inside tasks, outside tasks, and never tasks. Trust me, it's fun!

8

How to Set Critical Goals

I ONCE DID SOMETHING very stupid while camping in a remote area. I was tired and the sun was going down, but I suddenly
decided to pack up my belongings and head home. The reason
it was stupid is that I had only thirty minutes to paddle a lonely
kayak in open water before dark.

That's right, I was on an island again.

I packed up quickly and pushed off from shore. *No problem*,
I thought. I only have two miles to go. I noticed a shimmering
beacon off in the distance. It was another boater who was also
delayed. I watched as he slowly glided into the boat landing across
the lake. Then I listened as he argued with his significant other
about how to properly buoy a boat to the dock so he could re-
trieve their trailer. I don't think they realized how much sound
carries on a lake or that I was paddling toward them.

Husband: Hook up that thing.

Wife: What thing?

Husband: The thing by the thing.

Wife: I don't know what you're talking about.

I could tell they were tired. Been there, done that.

As the light dissipated a little faster than I expected, I did what any expert kayaker would do. I panicked. I took two lanterns and placed them at the front and rear of the kayak and started paddling much harder. I had one goal. It was to *not die*. I kept paddling toward that wonderful dynamic duo in front of me and the lights from their trailer.

It didn't take long.

"Beautiful night," I said to the couple. They had calmed down and both smiled at me with that look that said, "You are just as crazy as we are to be out here at dusk" and with some embarrassment about arguing.

I pulled my kayak to shore, packed my gear into the car, and drove off into the night.

∿∿∿

Notice anything about my kayaking experience? I never made a list. I kept my focus on one goal, and that was the only thing that mattered.

A critical goal is exactly like reaching the light at the boat landing. It's the one thing we really need to do *today*. To call it a task is insulting to all task management apps. Critical goals always align quite nicely with our ultimate purpose in life. These are the goals that have the biggest benefit. They are not always difficult or complex, but they are always critically important.

In my writing, I sometimes set a critical goal to complete one column by 9:00 a.m. This goal matches up with my personal life goal to communicate truth to others. I enjoy the work, so it's easy. I know I will feel a sense of accomplishment doing something I love.

For example, I once wrote a column about Zoom fatigue.[1] People were experiencing a sense of hopelessness connecting only by video during the pandemic. My critical goal lined up with my purpose. That same day, dozens of people emailed me to say they were experiencing Zoom fatigue. The deluge of email was overwhelming but also deeply satisfying. We'll cover how to deal with a deluge of email in part 2 of this book. For now, know this: critical goals produce smart results. They are more obvious (i.e., they stick out); they are more fulfilling and pertinent.

I like to stack the deck of productivity in my favor. To write a column by 9:00 a.m., I never schedule meetings or interviews during that window of time. I always use a fast and reliable laptop. I almost always turn off the notifications on my phone. I use a coffee machine that brews a luscious fine blend every time. I also tend to seek more accountability with other people and tell them about my critical goals. I don't like to mess around. Like my desire to reach the shore on my late-night kayak trip, a critical goal is always on the top of my mind.

You can set multiple critical goals in a day, but most likely you will have only one. That's really the point. When you plan your day, a critical goal is the one thing you know you want to do and even look forward to doing. It might be horrendously hard, like building an entire presentation to give to the school board. But it will be fulfilling and rewarding in the end.

Tying It All Together

Getting lost is easy. At least that's what my wife tells me. I sometimes turn off the GPS and just wing it to find a local eatery or a gas station. On long trips, we share driving duties, and I suddenly *become* the GPS. It's a bad habit. I know Google Maps can guide us home safely, but I like to think I'm smarter and wiser than an app built by Stanford-educated engineers.

In life, it's important to choose who has our ear. A friend used to talk about whom we have given permission to speak into our lives.

As we covered in the opening chapters, we decide what has meaning in our lives when we follow a morning routine, and this is also true when we plan our day. It seems as if everything is a priority even when we know that's not true. It seems as if we have to "get it all done" when that's not possible. A plan your day routine, then, is the next step after a morning routine.

Marissa Mayer, former CEO of Yahoo and now an entrepreneur, says that making a task list is important for the workday but that it's rare when you need to complete *everything* on that list.[2] In fact, she goes on to say that completing every item on your list is actually unproductive and perhaps a sign you are merely trying to be a completist.

A friend and writer told me, "Adhering to a list means we only do things on that list. But we also need to think outside the box. Many jobs require working above and beyond what you could come up with on a list each day. Others require you to make work decisions on the spot. Are you going to go with the flow in customer service and help make that sale that just came up, or are you going to say no because you have to stick to your list?"

Productivity guru Chris Bailey echoed the idea of being a completist in an article for CNBC's *Make It* blog.[3] We tend to think the goal is to finish everything on our list as quickly as possible. But in the column, he mentions the concept *precrastination*, a term USC professor Dr. David Rosenbaum coined in 2014. It means that in our attempt to complete tasks, we do them quickly and inefficiently. We rush into tasks without solid plans because we're afraid of procrastination.

I can relate. I've explained my own wonderful bursts of extreme productivity writing fifteen thousand articles in twenty years as a journalist. Yet I'm also a *precrastinator*. I jump into things too quickly. I used to keep a running list of articles in a seriously outdated app called Plaxo and enjoyed counting how many were on my "done" list (about ten thousand articles strong back then).

I stopped tracking the exact number when I started writing for *Inc.* in about 2008 because I knew I would write at least one column per day. Instead of tracking the total count, I would sometimes ask my editors to tell me the total number of posts I completed for the month, usually at least thirty to forty.

Why do we care about lists? It's human nature. We like to feel a sense of accomplishment and purpose, even if we know finishing a task list is not quite the same thing as being productive. The theme of this chapter, and quite honestly the theme of this entire book, is to become intentional about what we do and why, to avoid the trap of completing tasks only because it feels like we're accomplishing something, and to free up more of our time for the things that matter most. When we plan our day, it's helpful to think about our true intentions and our true motivations and goals.

Focus on What Really Matters

In her wonderful book called *The Lazy Genius Way: Embrace What Matters, Ditch What Doesn't, and Get Stuff Done*, author and podcaster Kendra Adachi explains how it's better to be a genius about a few things and lazy about less important matters.[4] This matches up nicely with what Ryder Carroll, creator of the Bullet Journal, says about perfunctory tasks. We don't like doing them. Even if we use a "genius" routine, if it leads to an end goal we don't like, it won't produce any purpose or meaning. Adachi and Carroll are making us rethink habit forming. When you take the time to plan your day, you are calibrating how those plans match with your critical goals.

According to Adachi, when we care about something, we do it well. When we don't care about something, we underperform. "That compels you to try even harder. Welcome to being tired," she writes.[5] We're always striving to know the difference. Adachi explains how a routine gives you a soft place to land. Automation and routine, at least initially, become a tag-team effort. On the one hand, you can "check out" and do the routine because you know it will help you form a habit. You won't be as tired. On the other hand, you won't need to work as hard at habit forming on your own willpower, relying on motivation and goal setting alone. You'll reduce cognitive load when you figure out what you really want to do. A routine is the engine to help you form habits to achieve the most critical goals.

Lin-Manuel Miranda—the composer, lyricist, and star of *Hamilton*—once said, "I have a lot of apps open in my brain right now."[6] Here's the rub: planning your day means you don't have to think as much about your upcoming decisions. You can close a few "brain" apps.

Setting priorities, picking a few critical goals—they're all designed to help you think through what's important and avoid the grocery-list approach to productivity. Keep focused on what matters, and plan your productivity with purpose.

Plan Your Day
ROUTINE

Planning is an intentional activity meant to reorient your tasks, meetings, and personal goals. Most of us already make plans or use a planner, so this routine helps you reset planning to make it more about intentionally matching your tasks and meetings to your life goals.

▶ BEFORE YOU START: *Prepare*

Prepare by grabbing your planner and journal. Make sure you have access to your meeting schedule. (It's okay to use your phone or a laptop for that.) Organize your work area and make a show of straightening a coffee cup or your journal.

▶ MINUTE ONE: *Think Ahead*

Before you start any planning, ponder what is coming up today. Avoid writing anything down. Think about any tasks facing you today, any meetings or appointments, and any stressors or challenges. Think about whether the activities you have today match your overall goals.

▶ MINUTES TWO THROUGH FOUR: *Write Down Tasks*

Jot down your tasks in the journal but don't worry about writing them all down. Note the most pressing tasks only. As described in this section, write at least two inside tasks (those you own), two outside tasks (those you still need to do but don't own), and one never task (something you shouldn't do and someone else owns). Also write down one smart goal. This is one big accomplishment that matches up with your overall life purpose. Cross off any never tasks.

▶ **MINUTES FIVE THROUGH SEVEN:** *TimeBox Your Meetings and Tasks*

After writing down your tasks, look at your planner or schedule and jot down any important meetings and appointments. Use the timeboxing method described in this section. Think about any meetings you can group together. Do the same with the tasks you write down. Can you group any of them? Spend the last twenty seconds looking over your final notes and plans.

Take a Break

The decision is rarely the point.
The point is for you to become fully
yourself in the presence of God.

—EMILY P. FREEMAN

9

How to Avoid Decision Fatigue

A MIDDLE-AGED CEO walks into an open-air atrium at the headquarters of a large multinational conglomerate. Known more for their transistor radios at the time, the company is based just outside of Tokyo, Japan, in a ward called Minato City. It's 1980, so the electronics industry is still growing in fits and starts. Known up until 1946 as Tokyo Tsushin Kogyo, the firm started out making a reel-to-reel player about the size of a microwave.

That's right—long before Sony Corporation made high-def televisions and the PlayStation console, the media giant was known more for their audio products, including the Walkman cassette player introduced in 1979. Back then, the device was everywhere. The headphones were only available in two colors, black or orange. You could only fast-forward, play, or stop your cassette tape. Yet it was *remarkable*. No portable audio device with a cassette had existed before the first Sony Walkman.

The CEO is here to talk shop. How did employees collaborate? What was their secret to innovation? He had just returned from a Sony factory tour where hundreds of workers labored tirelessly on an assembly line. In the atrium, the Sony chairman,

Akio Marita, greets him and they shake hands. After some idle chitchat, the man asks a pressing question: *Why does everyone in the factory wear the same uniform?*

Back then, the idea of simplified production techniques and what eventually became known as *The Toyota Way* at a neighboring automaker in the same city were still not widely understood in the United States. Both Sony and Toyota were not viewed as particularly innovative compared to American companies like IBM. Yet the man kept pressing for answers.

Finally, Marita reveals the secret. The uniform created a bond between workers and simplified one aspect of production: if a new worker joined the ranks and did not have acceptable clothing, no worries. Everyone looked the same, so there was always a foundation of teamwork.

The man suddenly has a light bulb moment. He jumps on a plane back to Silicon Valley and decides he'd like to encourage the same type of collaboration and bonding at his own firm. Eventually, he finds out who created the Sony uniform, which was made of ripstop nylon and had removable, zippered sleeves. Designer Issey Miyake agrees to make a black turtleneck using the same material.

Unfortunately, the man realizes his idea isn't going to fly. When he introduces the new uniform, the employees boo and hiss. American workers are not eager to don the exact same apparel. They want to stand out. The man gives up on the idea of a vest for everyone at his company, but he decides to start wearing it himself. Eventually he orders a closet full of black turtlenecks and wears them almost every single day.*

That's right: the company is Apple and the man was Steve Jobs. "I really want to clear my life to make it so that I have to make as few decisions as possible about anything except how to best

---

* This story is based on real events recounted in the Steve Jobs biography by Walter Isaacson.

serve this community," he said later, suggesting that, in some cases, collaboration is easier when you don't need to make as many decisions—especially about your wardrobe.[1]

᠕᠕᠕

Decision fatigue is a common ailment, and it results from having to make too many decisions throughout the day. We work hard and press forward with one meeting after another, switching tasks constantly, but never take the time to rest. We become tired and eventually make poorer and poorer decisions as the day progresses. One study by Dr. Roy Baumeister in the 1990s found that our energy levels deplete gradually throughout the day. In the morning, we can resist a donut or ice cream but later in the day, not so much.[2] (I'm including this study because it matches up with my own experience, although some experts have disputed the findings.)

The solution is to take a break and regain our energy. When we do that, we not only make better decisions but we're also able to tackle more complex projects even when they are later in the day. Breaks free us from making more decisions (because we don't make any during this time), similar to how Steve Jobs wore only turtlenecks.

As I mentioned earlier in this book, we make about thirty-five thousand decisions per day. As former *New York Times* reporter John Tierney notes, "No matter how rational and high-minded you try to be, you can't make decision after decision without paying a biological price. It's different from ordinary physical fatigue—you're not consciously aware of being tired—but you're low on mental energy."[3]

Author Daniel Pink writes about a study on breaks from 2011. Judges for a parole board in Israel were more lenient and fairer after they took a break from their cases. They were also more willing to deviate from the standard ruling in each case.[4] Pink also writes about a study by Desk Time in which they profiled their own users. They discovered people were 10 percent more productive when they took frequent breaks.[5]

Emily Hunter and Cindy Wu did a study for the *Journal of Applied Psychology* and found that shorter planned breaks are better than longer occasional breaks.[6] Pink also notes that the highest performers in an office usually take about a seventeen-minute break and then work for about fifty-two minutes.[7] That seems like a long break when it's about once per hour, so we're going to stick with a seven-minute break.

Finally, Pink mentions a study in South Korea about socializing during breaks. It was found to be more effective than using the free time to check email or social media—or even to get a snack in the break room.[8]

I mention these studies because breaks are incredibly important. As we make more and more decisions, the quality of those decisions degrades quickly. By the end of the day, we've become slaves to our bad decisions. It's one reason obesity is a problem and why people don't exercise. We charge ahead all day and by the evening we plop on the couch like slugs.

Experts say our ability to focus on complex tasks starts to wane right before lunch and then all afternoon. One study by the Bureau of Labor Statistics from 2011 profiled two thousand workers and found that, in an eight-hour day, they were truly focused for only three hours.[9] An early reader of this book told me she feels productive for about only four hours per day.

Eventually, the neurons stop firing as quickly. For example, during a long writing session for this book, I stopped about every two hours to take a break, sometimes following my own break routine for seven minutes but occasionally leaving a makeshift office in a cabin and going for a long walk or a bike ride next to a lake. When I came back, I had a renewed passion for the subject matter. I made better decisions about which sources, notes, and materials to include. I was revived and worked much smarter.

When we work too long, we get stuck in what author BJ Fogg calls a *motivation trough*.[10] We muddle through our work as if we're covered in occupational slime, dragging our keyboards along for the ride. A lack of progress on critical tasks has a major impact on our workday, leading to a feeling of unproductivity even though we worked continually.

Some experts say we should take a break every ninety minutes, but productivity guru Brendon Burchard suggests shortening that by half. I've heard extraordinary claims about breaks, saying we should only work about twenty minutes before we need to take one. It makes me wonder if we should make the entire day one long break and forget about work.

"A break of two to five minutes every hour can help you feel much more mentally alert and energized for your work and life overall," writes Burchard.[11] As you know, this book suggests a seven-minute break as the right length—although I'm not saying it's the perfect, gold standard. Okay, fine, I am saying that but feel free to diverge slightly! I hope Burchard reads this book and starts doing seven-minute breaks instead.

By the way, Burchard is an interesting guy. He's a performance coach, and over two million people have attended his productivity courses. During meetings, he sometimes makes people stand up and do a breathing exercise if it has gone longer than fifty minutes.[12] That reminds me of how Mister Rogers used to start all meetings and public gatherings with one minute of silence to think about who has impacted you.[13]

There's a wonderful quote by author Alex Soojung-Kim Pang: "Rest is a skill."[14] Henry Ford, noting how productivity was not quite as high as he would have liked on the assembly line, suggested shortening the workweek. That's right, you can credit him for giving you back your Saturday; Ford is why we work five days out of the week instead of six. It's also why we work forty hours per week.[15]

∿∿∿

We know from scientific studies that breaks are important. A study by the hygiene company Tork found that 88 percent of workers liked their job more when they had an opportunity to take a real lunch break.[16]

In the take a break routine, I'll explain what to do during this intentional recovery period, but the basic summary is this: whatever you do, *don't think about work*.

I'll say it now and several more times in this book: this break is also not about clearing your mind. When you do that, you might fill the empty void with negative thoughts. Mindfulness is a misnomer anyway. It usually means mind-*emptiness*. Instead, a break is a chance to *not* think about work, to evaluate your goals, and to "shoot the breeze" doing something fun and rewarding. Sudoku session anyone? A break resets and recalibrates your day to make sure you're on the right path as outlined in your morning routine and (later in this book) in your daily debrief.

A break frees us from constant decision-making. Like Steve Jobs, we can focus on what is most important in life and have more clarity of mind. We don't have to wallow in the low-level tasks and decisions that plague most office workers. We can collaborate more and enjoy what we do.

Moreover, you can link the most important tasks and objectives you outlined in the morning routine and when you planned your day. As you'll see in the next chapter, breaks free us from the dangers of overfocusing on less important tasks, the ones that create tunnel vision. A break helps reinforce even more the idea of linking what is most important to you in life with your daily tasks to make sure you haven't veered off course.

10 ⚡

Stop Tunneling Your Goals

CHRISTOPHER COLUMBUS WAS A TALL, muscular man with red hair.[1] Today, he might have competed on a reality show for lumberjacks chopping wood, climbing telephone poles, and carrying tree stumps around. Italian by birth but a Spanish immigrant, he was constantly on the move.

Even as a young child, he would travel on short adventures. By age fourteen, he had already spent time at sea near his home of Genoa.[2] Later, he would join trading vessels on long voyages across vast oceans. As the rhyme goes, they were often blue. In 1492, he set off on a grand adventure. His goal? To find a trade route from Spain to Asia, thinking there was nothing but ocean and sky waiting for him as he sailed west.

But not so much.

Columbus discovered the Americas on October 12 when he landed in the Bahamas.[3] In recent times, especially during the Black Lives Matter protests of 2020, his legend soured—and for good reason. Scholars suspect he was a slave trader and a goldmonger.[4] There are even some discrepancies about his appearance—he was probably tall but not redheaded.[5] He may not have even been Italian.[6] Portraits from long after his death were part of a marketing campaign to portray him as a legendary explorer because there are no known portraits of him when he was alive.*

We can, however, make an educated guess that he had tunnel vision. He made not one, not two or three voyages across the Atlantic Ocean but four total.[7] He had a "take no prisoners" attitude about his new world adventures even though we now know he did take prisoners and possibly let them die.[8] A History .com report about his life says, "He became obsessed with the possibility of pioneering a western sea route."[9]

In short, almost everything we know about Columbus is likely fabricated except for the part about his obsessive attitude about his goals.

〜〜〜

Tunneling is a result of constantly pushing, striving after, and focusing on one goal to such an extent that even taking a break is unnecessary. There's no time for anything else. The mission always takes center stage—and the side of the stage, the audience, and the parking lot. Perhaps if Columbus had been more intentional and less driven, he would have found the Americas sooner. Hyperfocusing and tunnel vision can lead to repetition of tasks, constant meandering, and eventually a lack of focus.

The wonderful thing about a break is that we detach ourselves from tunneling and refocus our priorities. We see the forest *and* the trees. As strategic branding and design expert Philip VanDusen mentioned in a YouTube video from 2020, our brains keep working on problems when we take breaks. Often, as we mull over the problem in an almost subconscious way, we realize there could be an alternate way to achieve our goals.[10]

* The truth is he would not have competed on a lumberjack show today. Maybe he'd host a conspiracy theory podcast instead.

Author John Eldredge has written about what he calls *benevolent detachment*.[11] It means we hold loosely to some relationships and release expectations for people because that's a loving and faith-filled approach. I'd like to suggest that the take a break routine helps us create some benevolent detachment to our tasks as well. We step aside from them because, as I've previously noted, we've already identified our purpose. Our work is part of who we are but doesn't have to define us.

Most of us are overworked, tired, and constantly in motion. Humans have around 128 billion neurons in our brains, give or take a few million. Neuroscientist Lisa Barrett told me you would think those neurons would be less active when we sleep and recharge, but they are still fluttering and flickering away. Sometimes they are *more* active when we sleep than in our waking hours. Dreams tend to use as many neurons as detailed work during the day, and we can't just tell them to stop. It's why we sometimes wake up suddenly from a vivid dream and actually feel more tired. At night, our brains are working the all-nighter shift.[12]

A break separates us from the problems at hand. We see them more clearly and can even decide if they are worth tackling. "Coming back from a break, you may find that you have new insights and ideas," explains VanDusen.[13] Spot on! When we step away from hyperfocusing, we gain a new perspective that's clear and accurate. Drive is a wonderful thing unless we are pushing ourselves toward the wrong goal. Productivity doesn't always mean nonstop work. It can mean no work at all.

How do you know when it's time to take a break? Look for the telltale signs. These include a lack of motivation for tasks, poor work output, and fatigue. It might be too late though if you already feel exhausted.

Instead, it's better to take *planned* breaks. I won't recommend an exact number of daily breaks because we're all different. Some of us won't require as many of them, but a good rule of thumb is to take a break at least once every two hours. The routine in this section is not that stringent about what you do when taking a break, but does provide guidance on the time involved. I've been known to brew coffee or play the online game Among Us.

As the routine explains, a break should not have anything to do with work. It's mostly a way to detach from all tasks for seven minutes.

My Own Struggle

Here's the cold, hard truth: I need to follow this routine myself. There are days when I have to add the take a break routine to my schedule. I'll ask the Amazon Alexa bot to remind me. I'll write down a planned break in my journal. My wife has suggested hiring a skywriting plane: "John, don't you think it's time for you to take a break?" I probably wouldn't see it.

I've always struggled with tunnel vision. I'm like one of those windup toys for kids. You turn the crank and off it goes in one direction. My closest friends know I can fixate on goals to such a great extent that I forget why I'm pursuing the goal in the first place. This can be a blessing in business. Give me something to do—build a department, create a website, write a book—and off I go in one direction. I could join the boy band with the same name. They'd probably kick me out for being too driven (or too old, more likely).

Tunnel vision is a problem for people with my personality type. In Myers-Briggs, I'm an Architect personality known for being good at building things, often at the expense of close relationships. Still, the saving grace is that I'm *saved by grace*. My faith has helped me buck the system for people with my personality type and explore strange and wonderful new directions such as showing empathy to others and loving the less fortunate.

Until recently, I didn't know what caused the ailment known as tunnel vision. I sometimes mistook it for drive and fervor, attributes that typically help build a team or create a new product.

For decades, I thought tunnel vision meant I was hyperfocused on my goals at the exclusion of everything else and that was a good thing.

Author Dan Heath—as well as a host of other productivity experts—now has a new name for tunnel vision. They call it *tunneling*,[14] and it's not a positive trait. They put a unique spin on tunnel vision to mean *productivity in the wrong direction*. Maybe it's all a play on words, but I like the new term. It makes me pay attention to tunnel vision when I'm hyperfocused.

Tunneling, as the name implies, occurs subconsciously. It's what happens when someone with their head stuck in the sand tries to move. We don't see where we're going because we can't see *anything*. We're goal oriented, but it's only about those goals and nothing else. We tunnel because we don't want to have to deal with reality. We overfocus on a few key objectives because finding new routes is scary.

As Heath explains, "When people are juggling a lot of problems, they give up trying to solve them all. They adopt tunnel vision. There's no long-term planning; there's no strategic prioritization of issues."[15] I feel the pang of familiarity when I read that. Fortunately, there's a solution: distancing ourselves from work during a planned, intentional break. This pulls us out of the tunnel and helps us see the light.

Why Routine Breaks Work

Productivity gurus tend to downplay goal setting. They say the process is most important. Follow a good process and you'll achieve your goals. I'm somewhere in between. Goals do help to drive us and so does the process. The word *goal* was not common until 1920.[16] I'm not sure what people did before then, but we can imagine they didn't carry around an expensive day planner.

Goals are motivators. For someone like me who struggles with tunneling, goals are also important because they help me to divide up my thought processes and not stay so hyperfocused on one or two main objectives.

Taking breaks is critical, and not just for those with my personality type. We all struggle with tunneling to some degree. We might lead a team of programmers on a project at work or decide to charge forward with a new social media campaign in the marketing department, and that's all we can think about. Taking a break that's intentional and planned—and does not actually involve the break room as you'll see in the routine—means we can refocus, recalibrate, and reenergize.

〰〰

A curious study from 2018 reveals a pesky problem with goal setting and how we choose tasks. Researchers discovered that people tend to set goals that are easier and to work on tasks that don't require as much effort. I guess that makes us smart, right? We might book a hotel or plan a meeting for the next morning rather than create a complicated sales presentation. Our brains are wired to do easy things. We don't like stress; we like things to stay calm. If there's stress involved, we balk.

The study found we pick not only easy tasks but also ones that are not as important or even worth doing. There's something else going on here, the researchers found. In addition to stress avoidance, we choose easier tasks because when we finish them we can say we accomplished *something*. It explains everything you need to know about social media. There's an illusion of accomplishment, of "getting things done" even if those things are trivial.[17]

Chapter 7, "Do the Most Important Tasks First," was all about doing hard things, the ones that matter most. If you use that strategy to align your tasks with your life goals, taking a break is critical. A break alleviates the pressure, since doing easy things is . . . easy. You don't need a break from the easy tasks. Remember that doing easy tasks can feel like you're accomplishing something important when that might not be the case.

This is quite fascinating to people like me who like to drive and push constantly toward our goals. I often need to recalibrate and stop pushing myself so hard. Perhaps I'm making progress on the wrong things. That's why in the next chapter, we'll cover the problem of self-awareness. As you'll see, taking a break means reducing the number of decisions you need to make (because you are not making any during this time) as a way to save the decision-making for the most important goals.

In section 4, "Debrief Your Day," we'll explore further how to know if you're completing the wrong tasks. I've inadvertently arrived at a common cause of stress, depression, and burnout: driving and pushing ourselves toward the wrong goals. Only by regular, intentional, and efficient periods of self-examination can we reorient ourselves.

As writer Kendra Adachi notes, sometimes we just need to take a minute on our front step and breathe to remind ourselves what it means to be human and why we're even on this planet.[18] Maybe we can pause here while you do that before we dive into the next chapter.

11

Becoming More Self-Aware

A BARRED OWL LOOKED down at me as if I was encroaching on its territory.

I'm about the size of a football player, but if you're familiar with this species, you know they don't mess around. It was warning me to pay attention.

I was walking up the road at night at the Wilderness Fellowship Ministries' prayer cabins in a remote part of Wisconsin. I mean, it's *really* remote. The owls are so loud you might think a small child is hooting at you from up in the trees. You duck reflexively because, to be honest, nothing that loud should exist in the wild. I backed away toward the light and into my cabin. "Nothing to see here, barred owl. Go back to your business."

Maybe that barred owl made me jump because I was getting used to the peace and solitude of not having easy access to the internet. I was there to listen and to avoid the constant pings of Facebook. I had to drive two hours to Wisconsin for that to happen. No swimming beaches, no kayaks, and no campfires to burn marshmallows. I was in a cabin called *Whisper*. What did I end up hearing? *Worry less*. I was convicted about my own nearsighted need for constant control. "Let tomorrow unfold the way it was always meant to be. Open your eyes to the world." *Listen more.*

One of my favorite authors is pastor and speaker Mark Batterson. I've read all of his books, some of them twice, so I know he likes to bring up the Johari window, a self-awareness tool.[1] Here's the highly condensed explanation of what it is. There are four quadrants. The upper left is what you know about yourself and what others know about you. The lower left is what you know about yourself but others don't know. The upper right is what others know about you but you don't know (at least not yet). The lower right is the strangest of all. It's what you don't know about yourself and neither does anyone else.

Catch all of that? It's a fun exercise to think about. I view that last quadrant as the one where we must listen. The thing about a whisper is you need to be quiet and listen closely to hear it.*

Self-awareness requires silence and reflection. When we take a break to jot down a few random thoughts in a journal or to call a friend, we are creating open spaces for reflection in order to interrupt the normal flow of work. It's easy to silence your phone but not as easy to silence your mind. An intentional break puts the world on mute, at least for a few minutes.

Why Taking a Break Is So Important

The routine of taking a break is not about making more decisions. It's about making fewer decisions and avoiding decision fatigue. The goal is to give your mind more space to think and ponder. As with the prayer cabin I mentioned earlier, this separation from all work, tasks, and responsibilities helps you step back and look at yourself from the outside in.

---

* A quick sidenote: Did you know you can whisper to Alexa? She whispers back. It's downright creepy.

In the context of becoming more self-aware about our habits, the Johari window suddenly takes on new meaning. It looks like the following:

Johari Window	Habit Forming
Things we know about ourselves but others don't	Our current known routines and habits
Things we know about ourselves and others know	Current routines and habits we know and everyone else knows
Things we don't know about ourselves but others do	Future habits we can learn through routines
Things we don't know about ourselves and neither do others	Habits God knows we can develop over time through routines

Imagine a future version of yourself. You're in great shape. You have more time. You are not always looking at your phone. You don't check email and social media every few minutes. You're incredibly efficient and productive. Every self-help tip you will ever read provides the same advice: if you follow a process, you will succeed. Great so far, right?

Good process = good results = good success.

Your habits are leading to the predictable results in your life. As we covered in the introduction, process is good. Setting goals is good. Purpose and self-discovery are good. Healthy habits are good.

What's often missing is the *why*.

Taking a break helps you become more introspective about those desires, about your life goals. As self-help guru Napoleon Hill once stated: "Strong, deeply rooted desire is the starting point for all achievement."[2]

If following a good process or routine is like an engine, then we must recognize that the productivity engine leads us somewhere. A break allows us to see if the engine is heading in the right direction.

It often means we need to stop doing so many things.

Being Human Is Exhausting

Input processing is a fascinating field of study. It turns out we're all constantly "processing" other people during a conversation—sizing them up, noticing their body language and mood, and analyzing their behavior for clues. We're also *mentalizing*, which means we are always constructing emotional models of behavior. Cal Newport, the go-to expert in this field, has connected the dots between input processing and why productivity is so difficult at times. We're "on" all the time.[3]

For example, you might be having a simple conversation with your spouse over dinner, but your brain is constantly trying to predict what he or she will say next. You've essentially constructed a figment of that person in your brain. There's the reality of what is happening during a conversation, and then there are the emotional nuances of how you are feeling, what you're predicting people will say, and even what you're believing about them, which may or may not be true. The battery almost runs dry.

In everyday situations, we're constantly trying to find our emotional bearings. How are we perceived? Are these facts true? Mentalizing is a way to not only understand ourselves but also develop a construct of another person—who we think they are or want to be, and how that relates to us. If that all sounds exhausting, then welcome to the human experience.

This is why we need to be so intentional about breaks: being a human is exhausting! We're constantly trying to find meaning in everyday situations; our antennas are always out, trying to perceive what others think. We need to take breaks to alleviate all that pressure.* Your phone needs to recharge once in a while; so does your brain. It's this separation from tasks that helps you

---

* Feel free to follow the take a break routine right now. Most authors don't ask readers to stop reading their book, but maybe you've already processed enough information for now. After you try the routine, I'll meet you back in the next section on debriefing your day.

to see them from a fresh, new perspective and to determine if they are worthwhile. Caring deeply about tasks doesn't mean you obsess over them. You also need to set them aside sometimes and let them germinate. This is one reason some of my best ideas come to me in the car or in the shower.

The main point? You can't perceive whether your tasks are worthwhile unless you take a break from them. The following routine helps you do that.

Take a Break
ROUTINE

A break helps you step away from work and focus on something else. When you come back, you'll be newly invigorated and energized to tackle more tasks. By the way, you won't need a journal for this routine.

▶ BEFORE YOU START: *Prepare*

Once again, before you start this routine, find a quiet place away from coworkers, kids, or anyone else. It might be the end of a hallway at work or the laundry room at home. Find a place where you won't be interrupted or distracted. It goes without saying that this routine is designed to give you a break from all technology as well, so stash your phone. Plan an activity that will take your mind off work, such as doing a brainteaser, reading a book of quotes, or studying Bible verses.

▶ MINUTE ONE: *Breathe*

This step involves taking several deep breaths as a way to relax and unwind. Breathe in, breathe out, then repeat. When you exhale, feel free to do that in an exaggerated way. Once you have focused on your breathing for sixty seconds, you will feel calmer and ready to do something new and different for a few minutes.

▶ MINUTES TWO THROUGH THREE: *Think about Something Fun*

The best way to forget about work is to cast thoughts about work out of your mind. Start by thinking about any nonwork goals such as mowing the lawn or doing laundry. Mundane tasks are fine! If you do have your journal handy, look over any of the hope moments you had in the morning to remind yourself about what really matters in life. Avoid any tasks or thoughts related to work.

▶ MINUTES FOUR THROUGH SIX: *Do Something Lazy*

Now it's time to engage in something lazy and fun. Do a brainteaser like Sudoku or a crossword puzzle. Don't feel rushed. Read a page in a novel or one page in a magazine. This routine is based on science (e.g., breaks give our brains respite), but it's not exact. If there is any routine in this book that's not as regimented, it's this one. If you prefer to sit and doodle, that's fine. Use this time for not doing any tasks.

▶ MINUTE SEVEN: *Review Your Break*

When you're done, think about what you did during the break, even if it was absolutely nothing, which is okay. The goal here is to be intentional about doing nothing. If you reviewed some of your hope moments or what you'll do after work, make a mental note about how the break helped you rediscover those insights.

Debrief Your Day

I examine my entire day and go back over
what I've done and said, hiding nothing
from myself, passing nothing by.

—SENECA

12

Achieving Goals by Unlearning Old Habits

PETER DRUCKER, a management expert who counseled hundreds of executives and wrote multiple bestselling books, liked to point out that people sometimes work on the wrong tasks. He offered a piece of advice that may surprise you: "There is nothing as useless as doing effectively that which should not be done at all."[1]

That might sound familiar as you look back on your day and realize you worked really hard on the wrong things.

Let's review the three steps we've covered so far to transform your productivity: Start with a morning routine to record your thoughts and look forward to the day. Plan your day with an intentionality that links your tasks to your life goals. Take breaks to reenergize so that your productivity is not purposeless and so that you can take a step back and see if tasks are worthwhile.

The next step is to debrief your day. A daily debrief links these activities together and teaches you how to be more intentional with your time: open-ended journaling time, planning your day, and taking breaks. A debrief helps us determine if we're veering off course before we realize late at night that we spent the day in the ditch.

A major theme of this book is recalibrating and reorienting what we do to make sure we are purposeful in our work. That's not easy. Looking back on our day requires some serious analysis. It's worth it because we can catch ourselves as early as possible when we're running off course.

An important question to ask yourself at the end of the day is, Did I accomplish what I wanted to accomplish?

A good follow-up question is, Did the tasks of the day align with my purpose and life goals?

Sometimes, our tasks are superficial. We bought groceries. We vacuumed the floors. On other days, we make profound, life-altering decisions that change the course of our lives. We accepted a new job offer. We asked someone to marry us.

Looking back helps you evaluate your day and decide if the choices you made are leading in the right direction. This isn't always easy. Just ask anyone who has ever gotten lost. You type in the destination on your GPS and head out on a shopping trip only to discover you entered the wrong address and now you're lost. Everything you see looks unfamiliar. It can be disorienting and stressful.

Neuroscientists say that getting lost, especially when you travel, creates new neural pathways in your brain that can lead to stress. We're formulating plans, deciding which way to go. It's draining. Then our brains start to do some rewiring. That adds even more stress.

A few years ago, I was in Los Angeles on a business trip working on an article about the guy who invented most of the cool stuff you see in the movie *Minority Report*.[2] (Hint: it was not Steven Spielberg.) He had only an hour for me on his schedule. I had a GPS strapped to the dashboard of my car (back in the days when they were not on our phones), a flip phone on the seat next to me, and a coffee with a lid that kept popping off. I had to drive across town in LA traffic, and my phone kept buzzing like it was trying to annoy me, alerting me to text messages in rapid succession.

My stress felt like the fizzing sound you hear when you put a pot back on a coffee-soaked hot plate. There was heat radiating out of my temporal lobes; my soaked shirt stuck to the leather seat. I still remember the anxiety. I tend to be calm and deal with stress just fine. However, when the dog is barking, my phone is chiming, and I'm focused on an important goal all at the same time, I feel myself going into overload. What's known as "the flow" of focused work becomes a mental logjam.

Later that night, I spent a few minutes thinking about how I could have reacted better. Maybe I should have pulled over and bought a sandwich? *Yep.* I could have avoided some obvious mistakes—for example, I could have turned off the phone and tossed out the coffee—and focused on what mattered the most: getting to the interview in one piece.*

Looking back is important. It's not just hindsight. It helps with foresight as well. Where we've been often dictates where we'll go.

〰〰

In this book so far, we've covered three important productivity routines (journaling, planning, and breaks). Now it's time for some nostalgia. I'm not talking about the current definition of the word, which means to look back at your past with warm feelings. The original meaning is from about three hundred years ago. At the time, Swiss merchants were fighting a war and missing their homeland. An unnamed medical student noticed this caused them stress—what he referred to as "pain" or aching. The word *nostalgia* literally means "homecoming ache" when you combine the original Greek words.[3]

---

* By the way, I did finally locate the company, do the interview, and write the article. Whew! See note 2 in this chapter for the link.

I like that because when I look back at my day, I'm not always happy with the results. I sometimes feel the pain of regret or at least a sense that things didn't go as planned. I wasn't intentional enough. I made snap decisions. When I hold those decisions up to the light, I ask a hard question: *Did the choices I made help with my overall life goals?*

One of my heroes is author and speaker Bob Goff. The guy has an infectious laugh and seems to be quite the jokester. When I interviewed him one time for an article and later for this book, he had just purchased a youth camp for no apparent reason other than *it was for sale.* I have a completely different personality from him; I'm not an extrovert who likes talking to strangers at airport terminals. Yet I recognize the value of how he lives each day as though he has only one chance. I want to look back on my day and think, *I made a few Bob Goff decisions. I made every one of my twenty thousand breaths count. I put all fifty thousand thoughts to good use.*[4]

I miss the days when you could buy a movie on DVD and listen to commentary from the directors and actors. They often reflected on decisions they made and how they would have filmed a scene differently. We play those same mental loops in our heads. When we snapped at a hotel clerk and noticed her grimace, when we laughed a bit too long after saying something sarcastic to a friend and saw their reaction. We repeat back what we said in our heads and feel the pain of a bad decision.

The debrief your day routine isn't intended to be a loop of regret. It's meant to help you develop an attitude of thankfulness, to record those moments of gratitude and develop a lifelong habit. As Christian author Neale Donald Walsch writes, "The struggle ends when the gratitude begins."[5]

In late 2019, I wrote an article for my *Inc.* column about how it's easier to think negative thoughts.[6] I had read about the scientific reasoning for that and was blown away. Cortisol is a chemical that alerts us to dangers, and it's quite prevalent in our brains.

We are wired to respond to negative situations due to a fight-or-flight mechanism. It turns out we have to work much harder to think about the positives. I immediately thought about how it's easier to be selfish than to show gratitude. A quote attributed to Henry David Thoreau comes to mind: "It's not what you look at that matters, it's what you see."[7] Gratitude requires a trained eye.

In the debrief your day routine, the goal is to unlearn the bad habit of thinking negative thoughts at the end of the day, those tapes we play back about our mistakes. It's better to document our successes and then to think about the choices we made and how we could have improved. It's a way to clear the mental pathways for the next day and to start afresh.

An early reader of this book who tried the debrief your day routine said she felt the act of documenting a negative thought helped stamp it out, to give it less credence in her life. It was out of her head, recorded on the page, and ready to be dismissed or dealt with later. When she documented positive thoughts, they often outnumbered the negative thoughts by far.

If you're like me, you know there are many choices to make, some of them easy and some hard. As author Mark Buchanan has noted, we often need to stand, look, and ask. When we look back at the day, we decide if we walked smoothly or stumbled. "The good way is not necessarily the quickest way or the easiest or even the safest. Its goodness is that it gets you there and does its work as you go," writes Buchanan.[8]

13

Hardship Makes Us Stronger

MULLING OVER WHAT WE DO is important because, as we learned in the previous chapter, we might not be working on the right things.

I've found it's incredibly hard to learn something new and motivate myself when the tasks feel meaningless. I've also found great joy and satisfaction when I believed in what I was doing. There was often a decision to either focus on meaningful tasks or choose frivolity. At the end of the day, I could look back and think about the difference between those two. When was I busy doing nothing? When did I take the easy way out instead of the *meaningful* way?

I often wonder, *What if I could slow down life and analyze my tasks more fully? What if I could breathe in and out and keep track of the minutes instead of the days or the weeks? What if I could stop and smell the roses—and the steak fajitas as well?* Too often, I don't stop to do that. I scarf down the Chipotle tacos and collect the loyalty reward points. On to the next task. But as author Debbie Millman says, "Busy is a decision."[1]

Being good at something does not mean we are fast. Even in writing this book I had to slow down. I had to become more intentional and *practiced*. To listen carefully. I wasn't thinking, *How much did I accomplish?* Instead, I asked myself, *Am I accomplishing the right things?*

We often choose what is easy and predictable. The cushy job downtown, the nice car, the yearly membership at the gym. Most of us don't embrace hardship or try to learn from it as a way to find purpose. Hardship is not always a bad thing and can help guide us. *Right* is often difficult.

What if what we really need to do is accept a big change?

One week after 9/11, on September 18, I found myself unemployed and looking for work. It took nine months to land my first writing assignment. Back in 2001 my kids were quite young. You can imagine the adjustment for each of them. Dad was always at work—now work is always at home. At the time, I decided to put a desk in the master bedroom and often tripped over the chair in the morning. That lasted about a month before I moved the desk down to an unfinished basement.

In 2001, the internet was still a novel concept. I remember connecting with a dial-up modem because Wi-Fi was not widely available yet. Being productive at home proved challenging those first few months. We had a little money in savings and a small severance package. We had only a few months before things were going to get a little dicey.

I didn't have to look far for motivation. They were all smiling at me when I woke up in the morning. My wife is a long-suffering patron saint, and she kept encouraging me to stick with it. To make a living, I would have to work hard and not accept no for an answer. I had applied to several jobs but the economy was in dire shape, and I was still a young pup.

Around this time, I first started writing in a journal to collect my thoughts. I not only started the morning routine but also chronicled late at night how successful I had been during the day.

I didn't formalize the debrief routine until later, but it started to take shape then. I wrote out my hopes and dreams, my challenges and setbacks. I even remember crossing off the stressors, which is something you'll try in the routine later in this section (and something you can do in the morning routine as well).

The debrief your day routine was born out of this stressful, uncertain period of a major career change. "Obstacles are those frightful things you see when you take your eyes off the goals," said Henry Ford.[2] I like that word *frightful*. Obstacles can scare you, but in my case, I had to press ahead. I had to pay close attention to how the career change was about to unfold.

That fall leading up to Christmas was quite stressful, trying to piece together a few minor assignments. I wrote game reviews for only fifty dollars each. I pushed myself to do better. I applied this rule by author Tom Peters: "Excellence is the next five minutes."[3]

By March the next year, I had secured a regular feature writer role at *Laptop* magazine. Something clicked. I realized almost right away that this magazine was part of a larger company called Bedford Publishing. I approached several other editors at sister magazines such as *PC Upgrade* and *TechEdge*. By the summer of 2002, I was making enough to pay the bills. The kids, not to mention my wife, were thrilled. It all sounds so easy, but it seemed insurmountable at the time. I had pitched one hundred articles per week to dozens of editors for about nine months. There were times when productivity looked exactly the same as sheer perseverance.

Around 2003, I secured another regular role at Wired.com writing news articles and reviews. Keep in mind this was a result of about two years of constant effort in a basement with my desk on a cement floor.

I love this quote by novelist Louis L'Amour: "There will be a time when you think everything is finished. That will be the beginning."[4] That's me in a nutshell. I'm that guy. It wasn't until 2008 that I started writing for *Inc.* and then eventually *Forbes*.

I sometimes wonder how my productivity would have evolved without an obstacle.

∿∿∿

Productivity often feels like pressure. We pursue perfection but it will always be elusive. Perfect is impossible. Quarterback Tom Brady once said that the point is to make progress, not be perfect.[5]

Even when everything in life seems perfect—we are in good health and we have food on the table—it never lasts. We sour on the direction we're heading; we change our minds. I'll explain later in this book how I discovered the joy of mentoring young adults and teaching them to write and become professional workers, but suffice it to say, I had to keep paying attention. In the biblical story of Abraham sacrificing Isaac, it was a good thing he was listening when God instructed him to change plans.

How about you? Have you analyzed the trajectory of your life? Don't wait to look back. I stayed on course with my writing for almost twenty years. In the next chapter, we'll dive into why looking back helps you move forward.

14

Ending the Day
with Renewed Hope

IT'S BEEN SAID that in five years from now you will likely not change or improve without the impact of another person in your life.[1] You will stay exactly the same. For most of us, if we do change, it will be due to challenges and obstacles that help us grow and mature, along with the accountability that's so important for that maturity.

What can help you the most? Looking back at your day.

As author and productivity expert Michael Hyatt writes, "Strive to make time for reflection every day. What ideas really matter to you? What are you feeling? Give yourself space to think through your day, including your daily decisions, wins, losses, ideas, insights, and everything else that made the day unique. This exercise ensures you're connected to a bigger why and that you don't get lost in the minutiae of life."[2]

Sometimes we have to *remember hope*. We have to look back and realize there was a time when hope was alive and well in us.

We also have to work hard at simply *remembering*. As neuroscientist Lisa Barrett explained to me, we do not remember actual events.[3] Our brains remember the last time we formed a memory of that event. This might even occur during the day when we think back about what occurred. It means we are remembering the memory, not the actual event. Our brains are constantly deconstructing and rebuilding memories.

By looking back at the day in the debrief your day routine, we're helping our brains to assemble the events in a logical way and to ponder them and reflect on them in order to remember them correctly.

During the debrief your day routine you'll process the events of the day and record them. You'll recall your notes and solidify them day by day.

But debriefing is more than looking back. It's also a way to look forward. We remember so that we can make better decisions tomorrow. The good memories are those we should repeat. The bad memories are those we leave in the past where they belong, never to trouble us again.

∿

For those who believe in human evolution (and I am not one of them, by the way), there's a widely accepted view that the first Homo sapiens who stood up, started cooking their food, and reasoned with each other also invented the concept of hope. One reason I don't believe that, among many other reasons, is that I view hope as part of our DNA. We were created from the beginning to have hope; it's baked into who we are as a species. While it might be true that other "animals" don't have hope, that doesn't mean we invented it as some random contrivance.

Even though we're wired to have hope, we also need to work hard to renew that hope, and a daily debrief session helps. We can look back at the hope moments we recorded in the morning routine and think about how they came to fruition. On the other hand, as a few early readers discovered while doing the routines in this book, there were moments when hope was more like wishful thinking. The debrief helps us know the difference.

As part of the daily debrief, it's important to imagine a future version of ourselves, one that's essentially a collection of those hope moments wrought into being. We evaluate the hope moments one by one. We imagine someone who is kind and loving, who is patient, who cares about the hurting and the lost. We look back at the day and think about how we started building that person one hope moment at a time.

Our debrief also involves examining our moments of distraction. When did we veer off course in assembling that person we want to become, when we didn't quite measure up to the person with meaning and purpose?

I view "productivity with purpose" as less urgent, less about time management, and less about a perfect task list and more about syncing up what we're doing each day with who we want to be.

As we'll see in part 2 of this book, distractions such as email, social media, and mindless web surfing can detract us from that daily sync.

In his book *Indistractable*, productivity expert Nir Eyal writes that there was a time when the stoics considered a book to be a distraction from what really mattered—namely, working hard.[4] (I understand their point, but please don't put this book down.) In 1942, Catholic nun and activist Dorothy Day wrote in her diary that she needed to turn off the radio as a way to avoid distraction.[5] Jordan Raynor writes that C. S. Lewis thought newspapers were shallow.[6] Today, I blame Hulu and podcasts. There are countless ways to become distracted.

Author Brendan Burchard has noted that distractions can lower productivity by 20 percent, according to recent studies. Distractions related to deep work and mentally draining tasks can cut our productivity in half.[7]

Philosopher John Stuart Mill created an interesting thought experiment that is relevant for the seven-minute debrief your day routine. Suppose you could snap your fingers and suddenly become the future version of yourself. Some of us might jump at the chance. All of our opinions validated! All of our daily trifles suddenly resolved!

But we wouldn't know *how* we validated those opinions or resolved those battles. If we suddenly became that future self, we would not experience the joy and happiness of the resolution and the growth. As Ryan Holiday notes, joy comes through the resolution.[8]

In the morning routine, you jot down random insights and hope moments and focus on priorities, but at night in the daily debrief you'll look back and ponder what you learned and how you can progress, inch by inch. As you'll see, looking back helps you make better decisions.

For example, in the early years of our marriage, my wife, Rebecca, would sometimes ask me to do a monthly budget. I resisted and, to be completely honest, I still do resist it. It was a struggle because I'm not a numbers guy. I used to respond to her in anger and say, "You wanted to marry an accountant!" We had the same argument multiple times, which is perhaps one definition of a healthy marriage. We kept trying to resolve an unsolvable problem. Turns out, I am not an accountant.

Yet the story about how we resolved this issue is illuminating. We looked back at those days and those arguments and finally realized what it was all about: she is better at managing money than me. The lesson was not about me taking over something I hated doing; it was about me relinquishing control over our finances and letting her excel in an area of expertise. The battle was not about our gifts; it was about my control. I can laugh at this now, but I'm in good company. Pastor and author Chuck Swindoll noted once how his wife does "the books" and keeps him in the dark about their expenses.[9]

With your daily debrief, you'll look into the past, warts and all. You'll learn how to do things differently the next day and then the next.

Are you ready to start that journey of reflection and progress? To look back at your day as a way to plan the next one? Transformation awaits!

Debrief Your Day
ROUTINE

Our final good habit is the debrief your day routine. This routine packs a lot of details into a short time, so be ready to jot down your thoughts quickly within the time allotted.

▶ **BEFORE YOU START:** *Prepare*

Before you begin, have a journal handy. You'll review some of your notes from the plan your day routine as well. If you jotted down anything during the other routines, you'll want to keep those available too. Debriefing your day is as much about unlearning bad habits as it is about learning new ones, so it's important to be honest with yourself. You'll record what worked but also what didn't work. Your goal is to review whether the activities, tasks, meetings, and events of your day matched up with your life goals.

▶ **MINUTE ONE:** *Start with Thankfulness*

Jot down at least one thing you are thankful for from the day. This can be incredibly specific—one person who smiled and noticed your efforts. It can also be more general and related to a feeling or thought. Write down any successful tasks you completed, goals you reached, or milestones. Circle any successes or tasks that are related to your life goals.

▶ **MINUTE TWO:** *Banish Negative Thoughts*

Spend exactly one minute writing down a few negative thoughts, events, or occurrences. These can be tasks you did that did not seem worthwhile, missing the mark on a project, or getting too loud with your kids. Write down anything that's causing you stress or creating a challenge.

▶ MINUTE THREE: *List Your Distractions*

Long lists don't increase productivity, so in this step, list only a few things that caused distraction during your day. Did you scroll through social media feeds too much? Buy the sugar-glazed donut? When you jot down anything that distracted you or felt like it was derailing you, write down why that is as well. What caused the distraction in the first place?

▶ MINUTE FOUR: *Review Your Hope Moments*

Here's the fun part. In the morning, you recorded the hope moments that filled you with joy and felt insightful and groundbreaking. Jot them down again as a way to remember them. Spend some time reviewing them and pondering how they impacted your day. Revel in these insights.

▶ MINUTES FIVE THROUGH SIX: *Ponder the Day*

Now spend some time pondering the events of the day. Circle the biggest success or accomplishment. Cross off any of the distractions, stressors, or challenges you faced as a way to remind yourself they are gone forever, at least for this particular day. Feel free to put a big red *X* on them.

▶ MINUTE SEVEN: *Review*

Do a final review. Relish the successes and joys of the day, and express thankfulness for them either verbally or by writing them down.

PART 2

Stop Bad Habits

Obsessively Checking Email

The internet gave us access to everything,
but it also gave everything access to us.

—JAMES VEITCH

15 ⚡

Houston, We Have an Email Problem

IN 2015, comedian James Veitch walked on stage during the TED Talk conference wearing goofy glasses and an even goofier grin. He smiled in a knowing and sarcastic way. The guy has a distinct British accent and sounds like he could join the comedy troupe Monty Python.[1] Like most TED speakers, he carried a remote to click through the slides in his presentation. He wore a suitcoat, but his talk was anything but formal.

Veitch started by mentioning a man named Solomon Odonkoh. He paused for a moment to let that name sink in. Why did it sound so weird? Because it's fake. The person doesn't exist. He's a spammer. The audience murmured a bit and you hear some chuckling. Veitch grinned like a Cheshire cat and put his hand on his hip. "I know," he quipped.

The guy has an engaging personality and a wonderful delivery style, but the dark undertone of his TED Talk—at last count, viewed by over sixty-three million people—is that *we feel his pain.*

Veitch explained a conversation with Odonkoh through email that not only came off the rails but also fell into the ravine and exploded in a billow of smoke. The point? Spam is ruining our lives. So is email. We're wading through the thick primordial soup of internet-based messaging like Neanderthals in the Stone Age. We bonk a few emails with our wooden clubs, but we're mostly lost in a mountain of messaging misery.

∿

According to Statista, humans sent 306 billion emails worldwide in 2020. By 2024, that number is expected to rise to about 362 billion emails.[2] My guess is that after the first few billion we start losing count. Sometimes it feels like my inbox has about a million of those. We can handle about five or six things at once, but cognitive overload occurs when we start juggling ten or fifteen more. Our arms are full of grocery bags. Then we add a toddler, a purse, a phone, and a few small kittens at the same time.

We need a new approach. Obsessively checking email is not the best use of our time. A paradigm shift—seeing email in a new light as something we can master within a set time frame—changes everything.

I experienced this on a book-writing trip recently. I stayed at the same hotel on two different occasions. It wasn't the same room but it felt like it. On the second visit, I changed my perspective. I moved the desk so it faced the window. I noticed a farm field off in the distance. I saw Canadian geese flying low over the horizon. I watched my Uber driver pull up.

It was refreshing because I felt as if I had found hope again. I was "in the zone," staring at the geese and rattling off these words. And guess what? I only checked my email once or twice during the visit. I was in the flow. I managed my email following the routine later in this section.

How to Solve the Problem

Immanuel Kant is famous for this quote: "Wisdom is [an] organized life."[3] While the moral philosopher we met earlier in this book never had to check email, he was highly regimented in his approach.

That's the opposite of how C. S. Lewis once described our condition. We're all "running about with fire extinguishers whenever there is a flood," he wrote.[4] Think about those spam messages James Veitch mentioned in his TED Talk. We're extinguishing email by playing whack-a-mole with the help of spam blockers and email filters, but the moles are winning.

Not keeping up on emails leads to deep feelings of guilt and anxiety in work and in life. We think we have to stay on top of it all day. When we don't keep a clean inbox, we think someone will find out and question our productivity. Author and podcaster Jocelyn Glei says we need to take drastic measures to regain control of our time. We're lost in a sewer of email about 28 percent of the day.[5] She even suggests using a second laptop at home that does not let you access work email.

What if I told you we don't have to maintain a clean inbox? What if we worked on more important things instead? Investor Warren Buffett has said work often hinges on what we *don't do* and what we avoid—in his case, it's the investments he *didn't* make. A well-known story is worth repeating: He once told the pilot of his private jet to make a list of twenty-five goals. He suggested circling the top five. The pilot asked what he should do about the remaining twenty, since they are also important. Buffett said to avoid them at all costs.[6]

He could have been talking about our inbox. Most of our emails are not worth processing. The one from your accountant isn't that important. If she needs you to do something, she'll find you. Checking email all day is like launching paper airplanes in the office. You can make one easily enough, toss it across the room, and watch it soar. And yet, they drift away harmlessly. Most emails make you feel a bit flat and are a poor substitute for real in-person communication or at least a Zoom call. In the same way, there's no comparison between a paper airplane and a real one.

There's a reason for that. Email is esoteric. We transmit missives to people, but we never know whether they will land. We don't know when or even if those messages will arrive. (The technically astute know there is a way to do that using a verified email, but let's move on.) The point is we can't see the other person, we can't read body language, and we can't make eye contact or hear voice inflections. Email is impersonal by design.

By the way, this is known as *asynchronous communication*. Send and forget. We hope the messages arrive at some point. We don't know when or where the recipient will read it. We're shooting blindly in the dark.

If you say something in person (which is always *synchronous*), you might see a reaction and can then apologize and explain why you were in a bad mood. If you send too many emails, it's considered spam. If you send even more, it's considered being productive. If you write an email that's too long, no one will read it. If your email is too short, it can lead to confusion.

Which means every email is just waiting to be misunderstood.

Fortunately, you can become productive with email, but it requires setting limits, using email effectively, and not overemphasizing it. The email routine described later in this section helps you tame the beast.

Enter the Email Routine

The seven-minute email routine is based on science. Not only is there evidence to suggest we're processing email incorrectly; there is also a scientific principle behind my email method. It's all about limiting how often you check for messages.

In everything you do at work or in life, it's far more efficient to follow one of the best productivity tips ever invented known as the "touch it once" principle. It comes from the world of analog paper pushing.

Before digital technology took over, paper forms ruled in the office. When someone dropped off a form at your desk, you either dealt with it right then, since the interruption had already occurred, or you filed it away. "Touch it once" means you won't have to go back to the form later.

Productivity guru David Allen created a similar technique in his book *Getting Things Done: The Art of Stress-Free Productivity*. It's called the two-minute rule.[7] If you have to complete a task and you realize it will only take two minutes to complete, it's better to do the task right then. There's no reason to wait until later.

Processing email is similar. We tend to check our email all day, but when we do, we create a circle of diminishing returns. We stop, check for messages, scan through them, answer a few, then go back to another project (or surf the internet looking for sweaters and shoes). It might be only thirty minutes later when we do this all over again.

It's a terrible cycle.

Author and professor Cal Newport calls this *attention residue*.[8] When we're interrupted and start a new task, our brains are still thinking about the previous task. Unlike Taylor Swift, we can't shake it off.*

Email creates a feedback loop in our brains. We check, send, check, send. The driving force behind this email obsession is based on a scientific principle. Researcher Linda Stone conducted an interesting study in 2012 about how our brains reward us with a dopamine hit when we receive a positive email.[9] We also

---

* Right around the time I was writing this, Capital One ran a commercial about making decisions. Taylor Swift walks to her closet full of look-alike cardigans and picks one. If you are keeping track, this is the only Taylor Swift reference in this book. You're welcome.

receive a shot of serotonin when we read a negative email—it's the same chemical that warns us about a hot stove or to yelp when we step on a LEGO.

Stone explains that we're suckers for this microfeedback. It's the same reason we tend to check social media feeds constantly, hoping to see if one of our posts is popular and has garnered a few comments.[10]

In the real world, we might receive a dopamine hit when we bike for several miles and make it back home or when we give a sales presentation at work and hundreds of people give us a standing ovation. However, the reward for email is shallow and insufficient. It's not real.

Seeing that the boss finally responded to our proposal about adding a fruit basket to the break room to encourage healthy eating? We might experience the same sense of mild euphoria from the dopamine, but it's not the same as completing a marathon. But our brains don't realize this. We feel the same sense of accomplishment when we score a goal in a virtual soccer game sitting on a couch eating chips and salsa.

We constantly crave these microrewards. The more we check email and see success in our messaging activities, the more we crave the reward. The cycle repeats again and again, all day. In case you're wondering, *yes, it sounds like obsession.* One definition of *obsession* from physician Vincent Felitti is "a constant pursuit of something that is just barely out of our grasp."[11] He might have been talking about email.

Email will never fill a void; it will never satisfy our desire for close human contact or resolve broken relationships. Those things happen in person. If there is a computer or a phone involved, real-life problems won't be resolved. As we'll explore, setting parameters on email helps reclaim many lost hours. Experts even know the exact amount of time you can reclaim.

16

Reclaim Thirty Hours of Work

MOST OF US HAVE a love-hate relationship with email. We know it's part of life, but few of us like processing it all day. The boss sends us a message late at night. We hop right on it because that's how we think productivity works. A few emails go to the spam folder by mistake, so we have to check there. Many of our emails are mundane, boring, stale, and annoying. The more email we receive, the more time we invest in decluttering our inbox.

In 2015, I made a glorious prediction that proved to be (mostly) true. Let me pause to pat my own back and feed my own ego. Okay, I'm done now.

I predicted the death of email about six years ago.[1] It's not quite dead yet in late 2020, but I was right about one thing: entire companies now rely on collaborative messaging apps like Slack instead of email. Employees seem happy about it. I'm calling that a success because email is not the primary form of communication. (I have to fess up that this is only true within certain teams and for certain types of discussions.)

When I first wrote about email reaching this comatose state, mostly for my *Inc.* column, readers agreed and gave each other high fives—or so I imagined. The king is dead, long live the king! Millions of people applauded the prediction, although some of them congratulated my pronouncement by sending me an email. I wrote #irony in reply.

Others were not so happy. Writing about the death of a messaging system beloved by those who use it as a marketing tool, for example, created some tension. One of my favorite exchanges occurred on Twitter of all places. I posted a link to my article predicting the dire state of email as a go-to platform, and someone kept arguing with me about it. After a few messages, the person realized he was arguing about email using a platform that's far more efficient when it comes to quick conversations and discussions. I'm sure he couldn't find my email address, right?

I decided to poke around with some collaboration experts and ask them why email is still a necessary evil, and the consensus was clear: it's because we're not very good at processing it. During a phone call with Wayne Kurtzman, a researcher at the analyst firm IDC, I asked about how email is destroying productivity.[2] I almost choked on my own email address when he told me about the results of a recent survey. He said that when modern workers rely more on collaborative apps like Slack, they reclaim thirty hours of work per week. I couldn't believe it—so I emailed him.

"Wayne, can you tell me that again?" I wrote.

"Yes, we can regain 30 hours! Collaboration is a team sport, and email is not. Email is a collection of personal silos of information that is hard to find and near impossible to effectively organize," he emailed back.*

Then I found another survey from Adobe, the company famous for making the Photoshop image editing app and many other tools. I wondered if a second survey might negate or disprove the IDC results. When I read the findings, I had to stop and pause for a moment. Adobe *also* found people spend thirty

* The irony of this email exchange is not lost on me.

hours per week chasing their email.[3] The plot thickens! That's about six hours per day. My goodness. It's no wonder computer scientist Cal Newport wrote an entire book about email ruining the workplace.[4]

In the same way that my morning routine takes seven minutes and my intentional break time lasts the same length, I tend to check email in short productive spurts. I'm lightning fast. Fingers clicking on the keyboard, swiping on my phone, tapping out replies—it's like watching a pro gamer use an Xbox controller minus the bazookas and total carnage.

For about seven minutes, I'm on fire. I spend the time weeding through messages and then move on to other tasks. We anticipate the conflicts, the drama, the lack of resolution. We get angry and sad. Newport says email is a terrible platform for dealing with the emotional nuances of life. This type of messaging seems to create emotional disconnection instead.

Author and productivity expert Chris Bailey has a theory about why that is. We experience attention overload and become zombielike as we browse email and leave too many of them unopened.[5]

That's one reason why in the email app Superhuman, the default interface shows only one email at a time and not a list. The creators of the app insist that's the best way to deal with your messages to avoid overload. It confirms Bailey's point—email demands too much attention.

There's an irony here. The British journalist Oliver Burkeman has a famous quote about the modern workplace: "Your attention is being spammed all day."[6] We think our inbox contains the important messages and the rest disappear. We never have to read about the Nigerian prince and his great need for financial support. Yet all email seems like spam after a while. It's one reason the Center for Creative Leadership says most people now work seventy-two hours per week on average.[7] We're hooked on email like fish.

Cal Newport goes to great lengths to avoid email. He doesn't have a public email address that actually reaches him. In a podcast interview with wellness expert Rich Roll, he explained how an unnamed Stanford researcher he knows doesn't even have an email address. He doesn't want to "stay on top of things" and prefers to focus on his research. He has a public mailing address instead. To contact him, you have to mail a letter, which his assistant gathers for him and puts in his physical inbox.[8]

Science-fiction author Neal Stephenson also doesn't use email. He has explained that he wants to focus on writing and not correspondence, to deal with his most relevant and immediate concerns. He tells readers he is more productive that way. He doesn't want you to bother him.[9]

Most of us don't have that luxury. Email is required in an office setting. Yet we can relegate email to a place of lesser prominence. To do that, to reclaim thirty hours of work per week, a good first step is to conduct an experiment to see how reliant you are on the medium.

The experiment goes like this. During an entire day, keep track of how often you check email. It can be just a quick second or a longer session. Track the total number of sessions you do at work and at home, whether on your phone, tablet, computer, or any other device.

Let's assume each session averages out to about fifteen minutes. If you check email twenty times per day, far below what is typical for most office workers, that's five hours of messaging per day. Assuming you do this each day of the week and a little on the weekend, that's thirty hours.

I'm here to say you can win this battle. I know because I did. In the next chapter, you'll take an email challenge to measure how much productivity loss this messaging platform is causing. For now, it's enough to know how much time you are spending in a week.

〰〰〰

Around 2018, I started a series of articles about millennials and what makes them tick. One column mentioned that millennials tend to hate older generations, including anyone over fifty.[10] It struck a nerve. For an entire week, my inbox was bursting at the seams. I received several hundred emails per day about that one topic. It was a mix of angry millennials saying the article missed the mark, older generations agreeing with me, millennials saying they liked what I had to say, and a few lost Gen Z souls wondering why anyone cared in the first place. I was a little surprised, because I thought Gen Z didn't even use email.

I became slightly obsessed about this email influx but in a good way. Every few hours, I'd look through another new batch. It was a strange week. And yet, I decided to respond to the most thoughtful emails. I commiserated with the readers who said they felt misunderstood. I replied to the angry readers and tried to engage in a healthy discussion with them.

Here's the interesting part. At the time, I applied a simple seven-minute method to these email sessions, something I've been doing for years. I was intentional and deliberate about it. I set aside any personal reasons for wanting to read what people had to say about my article and simply started processing the emails in a way that was more about the results and viewing email as a task that must be mastered than craving the microrewards and dopamine hits. I was doing this so that I could reply faster.

It was incredibly refreshing to be more intentional about my email. Similar to my seven-minute morning routine—writing in a journal and jotting down concerns for the day in a more regimented fashion—that helps us be more deliberate with our time, the email routine helps us be more focused. The science of sustained attention span—the period of time when we are far more productive, efficient, and attentive that is the basis for this entire book—has proven itself over and over again.

I spent exactly seven minutes processing my email, then set it aside for several hours. I didn't need to constantly go back and check for new messages. By introducing new parameters to this common activity of chasing email, I reduced it from an obsessive and time-consuming activity to one that was more streamlined and enjoyable. That's how I've checked my email for many years: seven minutes at a time.

It's a freeing exercise. You become more aware of why you like to check email, but you resist the temptation to let that guide your actions—and ruin your productivity. By processing your email in a more disciplined way, you free yourself to do more important tasks. You'll find you can achieve far more in your job and in your life when you become more intentional and systematic with things that don't really impact who you are and what you really care about the most. Intentionality leads to more efficiency.

If you're serious about conquering email and freeing up more time, and if you want to set clear parameters, you'll have to start with a challenge that might be . . . a little challenging.

17

The Great Email Challenge

In late 2017, BuzzFeed reporter Katie Notopoulos published an interesting article titled "I Tried Emailing Like a CEO and Quite Frankly, It Made My Life Better."[1] The author claimed it was just an experiment. (I reached out to her, but she is currently on maternity leave.)

Her goal was to find out if a curt, somewhat rude email style made her feel more in control of her inbox. She started responding to emails in a terse manner, often with only a few words that made her seem slightly agitated.

"That's a hard pass for me," she wrote to a public relations contact. She mostly used her phone and stopped worrying about how people perceived her attitude. The curious thing is that it worked, not so much for the recipient—she doesn't mention how people reacted to her tone—but in her own productivity. She compared herself to Mark Cuban, the famous entrepreneur who also tends to send one-word responses by email.

"Allow me to recommend you give it a try," she wrote. "It has made me unspeakably happy to not stress as much about emails anymore by being slightly impolite and quick in my replies. I encourage you all to try it."*

∧∧∧

To be clear, I'm not recommending this. I mention the rude email style for two reasons. One, *the struggle is real.* I fall into the trap of being too abrupt with my email. Two, *there must be a better way.* I find it interesting that Notopoulos took this approach, and it made me curious whether she's still emailing short responses like a boss. Yet I'll be the first to say it's tempting. Why not tell people what we really think by email? Why not get right to the point?

The problem is that it shows a lack of empathy to the recipient. I don't want to be "that guy" who sends rude emails all day. My greatest recent discovery about this type of electronic messaging is that it's all about relationships. There's a person on the other end of that email address. He or she probably has a family, pays a mortgage, and deals with family issues.

How we cope with the deluge of email is important because the people on the receiving end are important. They are coworkers, bosses, colleagues, and clients. They are family members and friends.

While it's true that the younger generation relies less and less on email, according to most studies, they are in for a shock. It's a daily ritual in business and in life as we get older. We can't simply delete our email accounts. Mastery is better than abstinence in this case. Most of us can't just delete our email address, but we can use it more wisely.

Here's my challenge for you: before you start the email routine described later in this section, *take a break from all email for three days in one stretch.* You can set an out-of-office reply or delete

---

* An early reader of this book mentioned a neat trick. He said you can encourage people to be brief and polite in their email responses by crafting your message so that it requires only a one-word response.

your email app on your smartphone. Let everyone know you're doing this. Ask your boss if it's okay to experiment and mention you will provide an alternative contact method such as a phone, social media chat, or text.

We'll call it an *email fast*. The reason it's so important is that it will help you clear your mind and your schedule. You won't focus on email at all during the day or, as Cal Newport mentions frequently, perform a "second shift" after work to catch up on email. Here's how to do the challenge:

Decide on when to do the challenge.

Set up an out-of-office reply.

Arrange an alternate contact method.

Estimate how much time you earn back.

Note any observations about productivity.

Track how many times you had the urge to check email.

The email fast helps you think about what is important when it comes to checking email. At the end of the three days, you won't lose weight or pump up your muscle tone, but you will know what you were missing. You'll see how effective it is to communicate through other methods and whether those avenues are valid and worthwhile. You'll learn how email makes you productive and how it destroys your productivity. The point of the email fast is to reveal your dependence on it and to experiment with other methods.*

Similar to an actual fast, I recommend you ease back into email. After the fast, try picking one or two days a week when you allow

---

* If you take the email challenge and discover some new findings about your own productivity, send the results to info@sevenminutesolution.com and I'll share the results on my website (anonymously, of course). Relish the irony of sending me an email after the three-day challenge. Also, if you discover you don't even need email, then brilliant! Stick to other messaging formats.

yourself to check email. Don't be surprised if you stick with that plan. The email fast will make you faster at email.

I tend to respond to Facebook chat messages as often as an unsolicited email these days. I never send emails to friends, family, or coworkers. The email fast prepares you for a more intentional approach. You don't really need to check email all day, as we'll see with the email routine.

When you resume your email activity, you'll discover how time-consuming it really is. Most of us would benefit from a little white flag at our desks that pops up when we experience email overload. "Don't send me any more messages; I started drowning in them shortly after lunch!" Author Nir Eyal has a T-shirt he wears warning people not to distract him. His wife wears a hat to let everyone know she is concentrating.[2]

With email, we have no such tools. Cal Newport describes how messaging can be synchronous (agreeing to chat in real time over text message) or asynchronous (not in real time so you can read the message later).[3] Both can ruin productivity. He says our brains are not wired to deal with one thousand messages in our inboxes. We tend to think in an interconnected and nonstructured way.[4]

In late 2020, asynchronous communication became extremely popular. Apps like Marco Polo allowed users to send a video message the recipient could view at any time. In early 2021, the app Clubhouse brought synchronous communication back. The drop-in audio app means you have to speak and listen in real time, like a live audio conference. Cal Newport is hypercritical of both forms of communication when they distract us. We're consumed by either *asynchronous apps* that let us pay attention on our own terms but distract us all day long or *synchronous apps* that mimic real-world interaction in the moment but can be completely exhausting. We can't win.

These days, we're dealing with all kinds of digital communication more and more, but is it worthwhile? Is having instant access to messaging all day actually making us productive?

"Of all the things that can boost emotions, motivation, and perceptions during a workday, the single most important is making progress in meaningful work," write authors Teresa Amabile and Steven Kramer in an article about motivation for *Harvard Business Review*.[5]

Not only is email often meaningless; it's also goal-less and repetitive. It's a distraction from purposeful work. Not to degrade this messaging medium too much (perhaps I already have), but the main issue has to do with what author Jocelyn Glei calls the *urge to finish*,[6] and what behavioral economist Dan Ariely calls a *perfect reward system*.[7] While all you see is text on a screen, you never know if you'll receive a job offer, hear about a fantastic new vacation rental, or find some other nugget.

No wonder we don't breathe when we check email. We're breathlessly waiting.

Rahul Vohra, the entrepreneur I mentioned in the first half of this book, told me that his Superhuman email app purposefully doesn't have a way to refresh your inbox. Messages arrive on their own, and you can't trigger new deliveries like you are playing a slot machine in Vegas. Most apps allow you to pull down from the top or refresh in some other way. Psychologists call this *positive intermittent reinforcement*.[8] Guess what? It works.

Interestingly, this is true of all apps. In Instagram, for example, there's a reason you briefly see posts on the screen of your phone, and then they suddenly disappear and you see new ones. You might call that *positive ephemeral reinforcement*. I'm not in the age demographic for Instagram, but I fall for it every time and it happens constantly. I see something I missed on the screen, and then I crave more. Poof, it's gone. The hunt begins.

It's like seeing your favorite candy for only a second. You crave the taste, and your brain tells you to find more. Dr. Anna Lemke, speaking in the Netflix documentary *The Social Dilemma*, mentioned that most of us are in a constant dopamine-deficit state. We're in that awkward neurological condition of "just enough pain and just enough pleasure" to satiate us and keep us happy and hooked, mildly interested and yet never fulfilled.[9]

If you're picturing future humans from the Pixar animated movie *WALL-E*, stuck in a stasis pod and unable to walk because we depend too much on technology, then you know what being hooked is all about.

In a few chapters, we'll do a deep dive on the dangers of social media. For now, what email is doing to our productivity is troubling enough. However, there is good news: technology can be a force for good. Perhaps you're ready to accept the email challenge, to fast from email for three days.

Rest assured that email is merely a tool. Like all innovations, it can help us communicate effectively or it can distract us and turn us into lumpy gluttonous jellyfish. The game changer, as we'll soon discover, is when we realize there is a human on the other end of that email address.

The Real Goal Is Relationships

DWIGHT EISENHOWER never opened his own snail mail. During his presidency, he was incredibly intentional about choosing the tasks that mattered most. He established a chain of command and stuck to it. Someone would open and read his letters, and then prioritize them.

Obeying the chain of command, never opening letters, letting someone else prioritize the letters he did need to see—these all led to a comprehensive system called the Eisenhower Priority Matrix.[1]

I won't bore you with the details about how the matrix works, but it was mostly a way to uncover inconsequential tasks and to differentiate between short-term and long-term objectives. "I have two kinds of problems: the urgent and the important. The urgent are not important, and the important are never urgent," said Eisenhower in a speech from 1954, quoting Dr. J. Roscoe Miller.[2]

As author Jordan Raynor has noted, Napoleon waited three entire weeks before opening any of his mail.[3] Curiously, most of the correspondence grew stale and didn't need a resolution.

While he waited, people would address the problems on their own.*

One of the great dangers with constant email checking is that we eventually become a constant email checker. Who knew? We always become defined by what we do, even if being an email checker was never a life goal.

We're looking for hope and meaning in the messages we receive, and that's why it's so compelling. But do we actually find them?

The Buddhist monk Thich Nhat Hanh touched on this often. He said that before we make any changes in life—say, to our routines and habits—we have to stop consuming things that are poisoning us.[4] We are what we consume, he said. If we mindlessly surf the web, we will be mindless web surfers. If we are looking to social media or email to provide a shallow sense of well-being and purpose, we will become shallow and purposeless.

As the stoic philosopher Aurelius said, "Ask yourself at every moment, 'Is this necessary?'"[5] The short answer: no, it isn't. Not at all.

The Person at the Other End

One secret to releasing the grip of email is to realize who is involved.

Each time you send or receive an email, remember that there is a living person sending and receiving messages (unless it's spam, of course). If the person who sent the email is sitting next to you, have a conversation instead.

Someone decided to string a few words together and compose a message intended for you. Avoiding the entire topic of email marketing and how millions of messages transmit over the internet

---

* This is similar to a leadership concept an early reader of this book called *strategic absence*. At times, an immediate response or constant supervision and overlording doesn't work.

each day trying to sell us products and services, know this: *most of your email involves humans.*

That means it's worth being intentional about messaging. Every person counts.

Author and pastor John Mark Comer answers email only one day of the week.[6] Why is that? He's trying to be intentional. He wants to process email not for the mere illusion of work and productivity. The higher goal is to connect and communicate with real people. It's a double benefit. You see email as more about people. Then you process the email in a more intentional way, which means you have more time for people.

∿∿∿

I found a higher calling and started viewing people as more than an email address in late 2016. Before that, full disclosure: I have known some of my editors for more than a decade but communicated only by email. In my defense, that's how the industry works. An editor makes an assignment and you deliver. As a journalist, delivering the goods mattered most.

My wife found a listing to help out at a Bible college in my state. I didn't think much about the opportunity and it was only a few hours per week, but I sent an email anyway. I honestly didn't expect to hear back. Eventually, someone responded, and next thing I knew I was doing some mentoring with college students, teaching them about the communications field. It was all remote at first, but as these things sometimes go, we ended up moving to be closer to the college. And then my role changed.

I helped start a student marketing team on the side while still writing my columns. Something changed in me. For so many years, I'd sent emails as a quick and efficient way to communicate with strangers. The students, though, were not strangers. One was my daughter. Others became my friends. Eventually, I mentored a group of about thirty students.

We rarely sent emails to each other. In about a four-year period, I sent only a few dozen emails to students. Most of the time, I met them in my office, sent instant messages and texts, or made phone calls. Why the about-face? What was motivating me to interact at a whole new level? During that time, my view of email changed dramatically. It used to be an asynchronous tool. In my writing career, it was invaluable as a way to pitch articles.

But in my mentoring role, emailing was not as effective. The students on the other end of my emails weren't that interested. They were facing major life decisions. In the same way you would not discuss a mortgage or plan a wedding by email, I was constantly trying to connect on a more personal and emotional level with the students. (If you have arranged a mortgage entirely by email, good for you. During the COVID pandemic, my daughter planned her wedding by email.)

The point here is that email doesn't have to rule the day. It can be effective for some communication. I'd never email my wife, which says a lot. We've overemphasized a messaging tool that is marginally effective.

My Biggest Email Mistake

Sadly, one of my biggest mistakes in the workplace involved email. Even today, I still feel a pang of regret.

Early in my corporate career, I was a hard-charging middle manager. Like a bull in a china shop wearing shoulder pads and a helmet, I had an abrupt communication style. I thought I was being decisive. (In my defense, I was also barely out of college.) One day, a programmer in the department sent me a sarcastic email. I can't recall the exact wording, but the not-so-subtle implication was that I had no idea what I was talking about.

"Why do you even work here?" I asked him in an abrupt and abrasive reply. Ouch! I instantly regretted sending it. To this day, I wish I had walked over to his desk and apologized for being a jerk. I was on the fast track at the company and tried to ignore my response. Yet days later, we had a blowout with his boss and my boss. I finally did apologize, but only after realizing it was not serving me well being so abrupt and rude.

What was I thinking? Obviously, that was the problem. *I wasn't thinking.* I didn't consider how there was a real human being sitting a few cubicles away from me.

∧∧∧

I'd like to say I've mastered this messaging platform since my corporate days, but not so much. I still sometimes send curt emails that get right to the point but that miss the whole point about personal interaction entirely. This book is built around the routines and practices I use in my own daily work because I need them as much as anyone.

Have you ever done this? You type up your terrible thoughts and then delete them.* Maybe that's okay and maybe it helps, but the original intention lingers. Following an email routine helps you think through what you're sending and why. As Eisenhower said, the urgent is seldom important.[7] Of the communication channels, email should be the most reasoned way to gather your thoughts and calibrate your tone.

More importantly, an email routine helps you determine if email is the best method for realizing your most important goals and ambitions in life. Maybe it's better to walk over to someone's desk or to call them by phone.

In the end, email either helps you become productive or becomes yet another distraction among many others. It should not be something you check constantly all day long. It doesn't have to inhibit your day. To be purposeful in your productivity means using the tools at your disposal wisely, efficiently, and intentionally. Now let's dig into the email routine and see how that all works in practice.

* If you do this, here's a hot tip: don't type their email address. That way you won't accidentally send it.

Email
ROUTINE

This routine puts email in its place. When you are done doing the routine, close out of your email entirely.

▶ BEFORE YOU START: *Prepare*

Start by taming your distractions. Turn off notifications and disable the ringer on your phone, close all those tabs you have running in your browser, and close out of any social media apps. Let coworkers around you or your spouse at home know you are checking email. Do anything you can to focus on email for the next seven minutes and nothing else, which will encourage more productivity.

▶ MINUTE ONE: *Scan*

Open your email (since you should always keep email closed at other times) on your phone or in a browser window. Quickly scan through all new messages and remind yourself why you have a few strays here and there. Flag the important messages (most email apps allow you to do this). Don't spend more than sixty seconds flagging messages. Mostly, determine what you are facing. How many new emails do you have? How many can you delete?

▶ MINUTE TWO: *Purge*

Ah yes, the great email purge. This is the most important step. Move quickly and delete unnecessary, annoying, and spammy emails that somehow made it into your inbox. Label unimportant messages or move them to a personal folder—whatever you have to do to remove them from your inbox. Mostly, just delete the ones that don't belong there.

▶ MINUTES THREE THROUGH FOUR: *Send Short Replies*

Go ahead and deal with a few of the important messages for two minutes. Start by labeling or organizing emails that deserve more immediate attention—meaning you shouldn't send an email but instead call on the phone, text message, or IM chat. Label them for a follow-up using anything but email. For now, only send short replies to make progress on this routine. Let the recipient know you will address a concern or follow up later. Answer any questions *pronto*.

▶ MINUTES FIVE THROUGH SIX: *Send Longer Replies*

For the next two minutes, send a couple of longer replies. Pick the most important messages (say, those from your boss). Don't labor over them too much. If a message requires a lengthy reply, consider making a phone call or scheduling a meeting instead. Off-load email chores when possible—for example, if you start to type a long email, turn it into a task to write up a document instead or even send text messages to resolve issues.

▶ MINUTE SEVEN: *Final Scan*

Do a quick final scan for new messages and to make sure your inbox is in order. Don't fret over "inbox zero" since that's a false sense of accomplishment. Keep important messages around and deal with them later. Make a show of completely closing out of your email.

Mindless Web Surfing and Social Media Use

In our society, those who have the best knowledge of what is happening are also those who are furthest from seeing the world as it is. In general, the greater the understanding, the greater the delusion; the more intelligent, the less sane.

—GEORGE ORWELL

19

The Great Deception

DOES BEING ONLINE make us dumber?

That's a question author Nicholas Carr posed in his wonderful book *The Shallows: What the Internet Is Doing to Our Brains* in 2011.

Unfortunately, the book has not aged well. I don't mean the information is not important or is outdated. I mean we're now *even dumber*.* Continually pursuing knowledge on the web and scrolling through our social media feeds has made us intellectually inferior and just plain stupid.

We don't need to memorize the meaning of new words; we can look them up. We don't need to look at a map and figure out where to drive; we let Google tell us. Carr explains how this cultural shift has created bad habits. Our brains are filling up with more knowledge as we surf, but the data is falling out the back of our brains at an alarming rate—and it's getting worse. We consume more data and we retain less and less.[1]

---

* There is great irony in the fact that the good habits described in part one of this book, such as writing in a journal and having a morning routine, are known to increase brain capacity and memory.

We're now racking up more Google searches than ever. In 2010, we searched Google about one billion times per day; that number in 2020 is closer to two trillion searches per day according to the website Ardorseo.com.[2] We're blowing the roof off mindless web surfing these days. According to data from Pingdom, there were about 255 million websites available in 2010.[3] Today, there are 1.74 billion sites.[4] For all we know, there might be 255 million sites dedicated to cat videos. (Actually, you can check yourself. When you google "cat videos," you'll see there are around 3.7 billion links. That's a lot of cats!)

So sit back, grab a bag of chips, and start clicking. It's a silly endeavor but let's have some fun anyway. It takes you about five seconds to visit one website. That means, if you plan to surf only one million websites it would take about 158 years. The math is revealing here. It would take hundreds and hundreds of years to visit 1.74 billion sites. The point is that it's impossible. There is too much information.

"The brain's capacity is not limited," Carr wrote in a new introduction to his book. "The passageway from perception to understanding is narrow. It takes patience and concentration to evaluate new information—to gauge the accuracy, to weigh its relevance and worth, to put it into context—and the internet, by design, subverts patience and concentration."[5]

Author John Eldredge has called this "the constant barrage of the trivial." He notes in his amazing book *Get Your Life Back: Everyday Practices for a World Gone Mad* that higher brain functions such as perception and empathy toward others develop in the brain at a slow pace.[6] Carr estimates that about half of our waking life today is spent staring at screens. It's no wonder we're all a little less engaged with each other. We're frantic about clicking all day, but as Carr notes, we now spend only six minutes per day reading books.[7] Hopefully you spend more time reading this one!

What Is Knowledge?

A question worth asking is, Why do we even care?

We live in an age when no task is ever fully completed. We don't revel anymore. There's always another website. Every click leads to another click. We're continually accumulating superficial knowledge we'll never use. It creates a constant state of superficiality.

Does all this surface knowledge make us smarter? Not really. More information leads to more noise. It's swirling all around us. Whatever we're experiencing—tech obsession, morbid obesity, drug use, marital woes—the solution we have picked of mindlessly surfing is not working.

In Greek, there are two words for *knowledge*. I'll spare you the actual Greek terms, but cutting to the chase, one word for *know* means an accumulation of knowledge. We know our own email address and phone number. We know the neighbor works for Homeland Security. (At least, I think he does; he even carries a revolver with him when he takes out the trash.) We know the names of our kids, the gerbil, the dog, and the cat. Some of us would like to forget we have a cat, but that's another story.*

The second type of *know* is far more interesting. The Greek word for this type of knowing implies *intimate knowledge*. I know and understand my wife and how she enjoys spending time with family, takes too long blow-drying her hair in the morning, and makes the most awesome broccoli sausage dish you'll ever taste. I'm not talking about facts and figures.

Sadly, web surfing always involves the first kind of knowing. Every new website creates more noise and more preoccupation. "Being busy does not always mean real work," wrote Thomas Edison.[8] This from a guy who never even used Google Chrome.

---

* My wife tamed a feral cat during the pandemic. We named it Never because I decided we would never let it in the house. It's sitting next to me right now as I write this.

We like the clicks. We think the furious flutter of websites is the same as productivity. The curious question for the age is, Why in the world do we like the web so much? The great deception of web surfing is that we're not getting smarter after all.

Why Do We Spend So Much Time Online?

Like all bad habits, we honestly don't know why we web surf and use social media so often. It's a reckless abandon to wasted time. By going online in a mindless state and visiting the same old sites and apps, we develop a habit of shallow repetition. We check Buzzfeed even when we know it's mindless drivel. We check Twitter and come up for air many hours later.

The perceived value of an activity or task should drive what we do. It should motivate our behavior. With the web, it doesn't seem to work that way. We gravitate toward valueless activities and tasks. The lack of any value drives what we do. Maybe that's the point: driving nowhere.

Time is short and everything we do matters. Living with intention means going far beyond mere self-development and mindfulness about our inner emotions and thoughts. The tasks we do each day should match up with our underlying purpose, as we covered in the first part of this book. Visiting that favorite Pinterest website is not wrong; spending another three hours looking at tree ornaments sure is. It's probably not even Christmas.

Our time on the web should be intentional so that we can quickly complete our tasks and then move back into the real world where we can make a difference. Vapid web surfing won't provide fulfillment, so developing better browsing habits makes sense. More intentional web browsing also addresses a serious workplace problem: we're not really working when we're surfing. According to one study by Kronos Incorporated, many of us are engaged in what they call *fake work*. Half of what we do each day doesn't advance the mission or purpose of the company.[9]*

When we free up more time for things that matter in life, we live with a greater sense of joy and purpose. We don't have to worry about success or pursuing more knowledge or more facts. As Rabbi Abraham Heschel said, "Never once in my life did I ask God for success or wisdom or power or fame. I asked for wonder, and he gave it to me."[10]

How do we find wonder at work? It's not on the web. IDC estimates the average office worker spends about 30 percent of their time searching for information on the web. That's two and a half hours per day.[11] Interact Source found that employees spend about 20 percent of their time trying to figure out how to do their jobs by searching on the web.[12] Maybe that's time well spent or maybe not. Employee training could lead to better productivity, but in most cases we're talking about employees trying to avoid work.

Sadly, we're not talking about purposeful improvement here. We're talking about what productivity expert Cal Newport calls the *hyperactive hivemind*. In a conversation I had with him recently, he explained how web surfing encourages rabbit trails. It might be our job to do web research, so we dive in on Google and later discover we've wasted countless hours surfing. We justify this type of browsing because the initial task seems valid. We let technology dictate what we do, why, and when. "We need to start by figuring out what is important and then strategically deploy technology in very specific ways," he suggested.

He then explained how being intentional with activities like web surfing, email, and social media starts with figuring out what is restorative and meaningful. We tend to do this backward. We start a search and let the technology dictate to us what is

---

* It's worth noting that being half-productive means we are not fulfilling our purpose in life either.

meaningful. "Once you know what you will use technology for, you can work backward and use it on your own terms," he says. "Some of us need to be really drastic. We need to stop seeing technology as a psychological pacifier and a distraction."[13]

When we search the web, we often fill our brains with useless information that leads to a false sense of productivity. Our brains hurt a little when we do this, but we can't stop. But are we completing any goals? Is that knowledge accumulation working? Is the salve helping or are we slaves? I'd argue that constant web surfing is creating hapless minions who don't know what we're talking about half the time. You know what a minion looks like, right? A yellow blob without a brain.

As we'll see in the next chapter, there's even scientific evidence of how surfing affects our brains. In the meantime, the main takeaway from this chapter is this: web surfing is probably not helping you do better work. There is a much better way to work by putting some guardrails on how we use technology.

20

What Happens to Your Brain When You Surf

I'M ONE OF THOSE rare individuals who has something called *selective memory retention*. I might have read about the concept in a book once but I can't remember for sure. It goes like this: the things I care about and value the most stick to my brain like glue. Things that are not that important—such as a dentist appointment, a list of items to pick up at the grocery store, or . . . a dentist appointment—don't make it in there (and by *there* I mean the big lump of pink tissue in my head).

Some facts just don't stay lodged in my synapses. Phone numbers, meaningless bits of trivia, the last time we took the cat to the vet. I'm being selectively retentive, apparently. I'm in good company. Albert Einstein couldn't recall his own phone number, and Mark Zuckerberg often wears the same shirt every day.

I remember the first time I used the World Wide Web. I even remember the site I visited. It was a gaming portal known as Games Domain. No idea why I remember this, but I can still recall the logo, the layout of the site—it was rudimentary with a few images but mostly text—and the name of the editor who ran it. (Richard Greenhill, if you are still out there, look me up.) Way back in the dark recesses of time immemorial, also known as 1994, I connected my computer to this new thing called *the internet* and typed in that domain. Eventually, I even contacted Greenhill and wrote a few game reviews.

My selective memory retention doesn't end there. I remember visiting Ford.com when it first debuted. And a new site called Amazon. At the time, I was a graphics design manager at a start-up, and to this day I remember the exact person who told me about the internet, showed me a few sites he liked, and helped me get connected. I also remember building the company website with him right around 1995 or so. It was a cool time because the technology was so new and exciting.

Fast-forward to 2020 and I can't remember the website I visited five minutes ago. It's a blur. Thankfully, I stopped mindless web surfing over a decade ago because it never seemed like a good use of time. Once you've visited the first million sites after Games Domain and Ford.com, it's all downhill from there. I sometimes sit with my wife, Rebecca, at night and browse a few websites with her, looking up regional parks and camper cabins. But for the most part, I've kicked the habit.

My secret is being intentional about why I'm online in the first place by setting a web browsing goal just about every time. I also know too much about what's happening to our brains when we surf, what tech companies are trying to accomplish, and why it's dangerous.

〜〜〜

I'd like to introduce you to a guy who knows all about this topic.

Tristan Harris became famous in 2020 when he appeared in the Netflix documentary *The Social Dilemma*. The former ethicist at Google once worked on a team that was trying to figure out how to balance the obsessive nature of web surfing with the company mantra at the time, which was "don't be evil." In October of 2015 they changed it to "do the right thing" instead. It was a delicate balance. Harris wanted to make sure people used Google. (Today, it's quite often—about sixty-three thousand searches every second.[1]) Yet he knew web surfing is dangerous.

In what was likely completely unrelated, he left the company about two months after they changed their motto.[2]

At that time, the brain science related to obsessive web browsing was still a bit murky. We just didn't know. In the morning, we'd wake up and flick through a few news sites. That seems harmless enough until you realize it's an hour later and you're still browsing.

On a *CBS This Morning* appearance in late 2019, Harris—who is a vocal critic of obsessive technology—talked about how our online activity is "downgrading humans" and that tech companies are "extracting human attention" from us. *Tell us what you really think* was my first reaction. Harris was not just talking about social media though. It's any app.

"It's a race to the bottom of the brain stem," he said. "It's about how many minutes [tech companies] can get from your mind."[3] Harris makes the point that those minutes equate to advertising dollars. The more time we spend looking at ads, the more money the tech companies make.

He's not alone in criticizing Facebook and others. Some of them helped create the problem in the first place and now seem to be backtracking and offering alternatives. (Harris talks about a *regenerative attention economy* where tech companies encourage us to spend more time outside or to give to worthwhile causes.) Sean Parker served as the president of Facebook in the early days and now talks openly about the dangers of social media and online obsession. At an Axios conference in 2017, he explained that Facebook is now a social-validation feedback loop. It has changed society, he said at the time, and destroyed productivity.[4]

Chamath Palihapitiya, who was the vice president of user growth at Facebook in the early days, seems to have deep regrets about tech. He once prescribed to the well-known mantra in Silicon Valley to "fail fast" because it's important to keep users hooked. If something is not attracting enough users, try different tactics.

"[This is] exploiting a vulnerability in human psychology," he said, explaining how social media companies lure us in and get us hooked.[5] Yet, he lamented our loss of control and how tech companies were not taking responsibility for how alluring it is to surf and use social media. "If you feed the beast, that beast will destroy you."[6]

〰〰

Why do we keep clicking then? Most of us don't really know. One study by Common Sense Media from 2015 suggested we use our screens as much as nine hours per day.[7] It might be far worse today, especially since the pandemic changed how we all work. A Salary.com study from 2014 found that 70 percent of office workers waste time on the web.[8]

I believe the main culprit is *stress*. We use web surfing as a coping mechanism. According to Stanford University research, we tend to switch tasks every nineteen seconds when we're on a computer.[9] We're trying to entertain ourselves with clicks—but it's not working.

Have you noticed this tendency in yourself? I don't web surf when I'm working on tasks I enjoy. I stay focused. Musician David Crowder says that it's important to do something so cool you don't need to use your phone.[10] I once asked professor and book author Sherry Turkle about the phenomenon of using distractions such as web surfing on a phone to alleviate stress, and she told me about how even young adults put their phones away when they meet with a banker.[11] Whatever power the web holds over us to mindlessly surf, we apparently keep it at bay during important meetings. Sadly, that was about five years ago. Since then, I've heard that people will pull out their phones even during bank meetings.*

Brain imagery scans of people who are addicted to web-based video games tell an interesting story. I remember visiting a company in Seattle that makes colorful brain maps—technically called *functional magnetic resonance imaging maps*—and marveling at how the neurons clumped together and how abnormal they appeared when I compared them to the brain scans of nonaddicted people. We all have vices but being obsessed with web-based games actually *looks* scary.[12]

We're data gluttons. Author Jefferson Bethke notes that the amount of information the world produces in only two days is equivalent to the data generated from the dawn of time until 2003.[13] That's a lot of data! We suffer from what author Adam Alter calls *persistent overengagement*.[14]

This constant influx is always on a virtual plane—our screens. In science there is a concept called *sensory dynamism*. It means our brains need multiple layers of sense input. When we look out the window, we see the window frame, the bush in front of the window, the lawn, and a house off in the distance. In the skyline, we can barely see a few birds flying low over the horizon. Our brains love that. Sensory dynamism creates a sense of calm because our eyes are wired to change focus. We like to look at something up close, then compare it to something far away.[15]

That doesn't happen with the web. Everything is one dimensional. Our computer monitors sit a foot or two from our noses. We are constantly looking at something that's near us. Those who work in an office or at home and can look out the window occasionally have an advantage. If only we did that more often. When we furiously click on websites, we are not experiencing sensory dynamism.†

* Please don't do this.
† An early reader of this book made a fabulous point. He wondered whether writers and those who produce web content should become more methodical

It gets worse. A lot worse. Constant web browsing, even if we're not obsessed, is pulling us away from things that matter. Forget the loss of productivity for a moment. We're talking about a loss of reality. Not setting parameters for web surfing is costing us *everything*.

This hit home for me the other day while I watched an indie movie called *Driveways*.[16] The story is about a mom and her son who are forced to clean up the house of her sister who died. A Korean vet and widower named Del who lives next door befriends the son. It's a touching story about kindness, but the final scene is what caught my attention.

Del is telling the son about his wife and how she remembered birthdays and would always be the one to make social connections. He recalls how they first met and explains how he wishes he could have the time back.

"Your life passes by so quickly, forty to fifty years are just gone," he says. If he could only go back and relive those experiences, he would be far more deliberate. You probably have to watch the scene to understand the context and pick up on the emotion, but it hit me right between the old cerebral cortex: time is precious; being deliberate *matters*.

Instead of living in a superficial way, constantly clicking, we can rein in our online travels. It starts with setting boundaries on usage.

---

and purposeful. Maybe we should all slow down. As others crank out hundreds of stories as trivial click bait, Christians should be far more intentional.

21

Feeding the Right Wolf When You're Online

A NATIVE AMERICAN BOY arrives home after school and starts talking to his grandfather. The boy is struggling with resentment toward another child his age. He felt slighted and is now upset and angry. The grandfather tells his grandson there are two wolves living inside of him, one that shows kindness and compassion and another that fills us with rage and a contentious attitude.

"Which wolf will win?" asks the boy.

"The one you feed," replies the grandfather.

I like this story, which I've condensed quite a bit, because it applies to our current predicament with the web.* It seems the angry wolf is easier than ever to feed. We click on a conspiracy theory site or browse to a news portal that presents barely factual information. If there's an easier way to feed the angry wolf other than simply clicking on a website, I'm not sure what it is. The web seems intentionally designed to fuel hate clicks.

* Okay, I realize the story about feeding the right wolf is an Instagram meme and might not even be real. I still like it.

Watch someone use the web and you'll see a flurry of activity. In Google Chrome, I've been known to run twenty tabs in a row, clicking like a crazed animal between them. It feels productive to switch between tabs even though I'm clicking, clicking, clicking all day on nothing. My mouse moves faster than my brain. I'm a superhero, the Flash with a keyboard.

Productivity on the web is not about the speed of our clicks but should be defined as *intentional labor meant to reach a specific goal*. Setting a parameter for our endeavors helps—for example, find ten new jobs by dinnertime, look up five new customers to pitch on a sales presentation before the next meeting. We set limits in other areas of life, why not the web?

Becoming more intentional about web browsing means we become aware of that insatiable wolf. We feed the good wolf, the one that satisfies our innate desire to be more efficient and time conscious. Efficiency on the web does not mean fluency or speed. It might even mean clicking slower. The web is not inherently bad; using it inefficiently is the bad habit.

I discovered how being intentional and proceeding slowly and deliberately works in spectacular fashion while I was writing this book. I stayed at a hotel in the Twin Cities and, for my breaks, I took long walks in cold weather. One day, I came to a bridge and noticed there were patches of ice everywhere. I had a few choices. One was to walk along the road, which would have put me in danger. (No one pays attention to book authors trying to avoid ice by walking on a busy street.) I could have turned back, but that would have cut the walk short. I decided to proceed *slowly*. I stepped on each ice patch with deliberation. I inched my way across the bridge.

This type of productivity matches up with what I suggest for using the web—slowly and more intentionally. You're still making progress. Browsing slowly or clicking with intention does not mean you are unproductive.

How to Be Intentional

As a journalist, I know that the temptation to rush through our work is real. I sometimes think, *Just one more article*. In writing this book, I decided to surf slower, to browse less, and to avoid mindless clicking. I didn't want to go down the rabbit hole looking for advice on the web. I'm partly to blame for this after writing hundreds of articles about productivity, but if you know where to look, you will find not hundreds or thousands but millions of articles. I went to great lengths to avoid the urge to surf.

Another step involved the remote island I mentioned at the beginning of this book. I wrote this chapter on my third trip. I decided I wouldn't browse the web more than a few minutes here and there. I mostly sat on a bench at the top of a hill and read books, took notes, and typed on a laptop. I would read an entire book to glean one critical detail. The process was slow, methodical . . . and wonderful.

When author Tim Ferriss wrote his famous book *The 4-Hour Workweek*, he tapped into a spiritual truth: it's more about doing our best than doing the most. Ferriss says we should work less and accomplish more.[1]

I heartily agree. I prefer to let the insights in my job come slowly rather than click, click, click all day. I prefer to slow down and listen.

There's a wonderful Greek word, *metanoia*, that means (in my own understanding of it) a conversion or transformation from one deep state to another.[2] I thought deeply about using the word as the title for this book, but few would have known what it meant. To move from one deep state to another requires intentionality. It requires purpose.*

The way we use digital technology should have this same forethought. If our goal is to be more intentional with our time and

---

* Most of you understand the word metanoia as "meta" (or *transformational*) these days. There are a few other words I'd like to reclaim from popular culture. One example: when I hear that something on the web has "gone viral" these days, it gives me pause.

avoid the shallow mindlessness of web surfing, our online activity needs more purpose.

Author Greg McKeown has noted that 40 percent of the choices we make in life come from a place of deep subconscious thought.[3] If that's true, we should approach every activity as feeding our subconscious in a way that's either healthy and helpful (the good wolf) or destructive (the bad wolf).

If we believe *metanoia* is important, we will be careful to be 100 percent present in the moment. Laura Ingalls Wilder once wrote, "Now is now. It can never be a long time ago."[4] Our ability to focus, what scientists call the *salience network* in our brains that helps us attune to what is important, will thrive.

No monotonous clicks for us, only *metanoia* of one state to another.

Feeding the Wrong Wolf

We have access to endless amounts of information, yet we don't have the tools to throttle our appetite. The question is, Why do we keep feeding the wrong wolf?

One reason is that we keep looking for quick fixes. "You see how few things you have to do to live a satisfying . . . life," wrote Marcus Aurelius.[5] Apparently, we don't. We think it requires *more*. The Big Gulp of online activity, the Supersize of Google search engines. Our browser history is a mile long and an inch thick. Remember what former Facebook executive Chamath Palihapitiya said, "If you feed the beast, then that beast will destroy you."[6] We feed the beast even as we watch it expand.

We don't like limits. Our internet runs at 1GB per second, but that's not fast enough. Our phones connect at 4G speeds; we need 5G instead. Faster and faster, better and better. Yet, as I mentioned, we can't transform ourselves from a shallow, surface-level state to something more profound with a click.

Almost all of us suffer from tech obsession these days. One estimate suggests we spend as much as nine hours and forty-five minutes per day using online tools such as email, the web, and social media.[7] Most of us are only awake about fourteen hours a day. We're quickly approaching total saturation of the digital realm. It's why a Netflix executive once said their main competitor is sleep.[8]

Feeding the wrong wolf has dire consequences. The wolf of kindness, compassion, and empathy is now dying a slow and painful death. We skim along the surface, hoping these activities will meet some subconscious need. However, the more we are trapped by these bad habits, the harder it is to transform ourselves and break free.

Before we learn how to halt our constant web surfing, let's also examine what we seek when we use social media.

22

Avoiding the Doom Scroll on Social Media

WHEN NIR EYAL PUBLISHED his book *Indistractable: How to Control Your Attention and Choose Your Life* in August of 2019, the world was relatively safe. The economy in mid to late summer was pumping on all cylinders (the GDP increased by 2.1 percent[1]), the unemployment rate had dropped to 3.5 percent,[2] and no major wars were raging around the world.

That fall, his book became a national bestseller, and Eyal, an author and speaker who has taught university courses and consulted with major companies such as Google and Microsoft, became more famous. He was an outspoken critic of how apps like Facebook and Instagram use techniques that are not that dissimilar from how a Las Vegas slot machine works to make sure we keep clicking, liking, sharing, and scrolling. (Another expert, Tristan Harris, uses the same slot machine analogy.)

That fall, Eyal used a term for how social media apps tend to make us form bad habits and become obsessed. He called it the *infinite scroll*.[3] Imagine a full-grown adult standing in the line at Starbucks flipping through countless photos of people celebrating birthdays and posing in front of beaches, and you'll know exactly what it's like. Our brains are constantly seeking these feedback loops and microrewards, even if they involve pictures of cute babies and teenagers showing off a new hairstyle. Eyal spoke about how these apps hook the user. His solution was to develop new routines and habits that help us become more disciplined in our use.

And then everything changed in January of 2020. The first reported cases of COVID-19 in Wuhan, China, took everyone by surprise. Some of us, including myself, dismissed it as a minor outbreak. It would subside. It would not make a global impact. We were wrong. A pandemic ensued. By December 2020, 1,639,088 people have died worldwide with over 73,712,330 reported cases. Unemployment rates skyrocketed to over 11 percent in the United States, which means about 23 million people were unemployed as of August 2020.[4] The economy crashed and burned, dropping by nearly 40 percent according to the Bureau of Economic Analysis.[5]

As you can imagine, this created a whole new level of stress. Eyal told me by phone that he noticed a quick spike in book sales during this time period, surprising everyone involved—especially his publisher.[6]

"We all started searching for some form of escape," he told me, explaining how the normal methods of managing our time, controlling our tech urges, and even scheduling our time tend to blow up during periods when our mental well-being is under attack from all angles. We lack consistency during these times, and we tend to use social media as a salve. "We all have internal triggers," he says. "When we're suffering and more anxious, we turn to social media to relieve the pain."

I noticed this change in myself. When I was writing this book, the United States experienced a surge in coronavirus cases in places like Texas, California, Florida, and even the Midwest. Meanwhile, my youngest daughter, Katherine, was planning a wedding, I changed jobs, we had problems with our house, and . . . I was writing a book. When stress happens, as it always does, we look for quick fixes. All it takes is moving your finger a few inches across the screen of your phone. Eyal told me distraction starts inside of us, in our hearts and minds, when we look for quick relief. We experience minor discomfort and click on Instagram.

My thoughts turned negative at times. I wasn't alone. One study found that people around the world send six thousand tweets every second.[7] The most interesting discovery is that tweets are more positive in the morning and then slowly become more and more negative. As the day progresses and we experience stress, distraction, and setbacks, we devolve.[8]

Author and researcher Angela Duckworth has talked about how negativity is like a virus. It spreads faster and infects more people than positive thoughts. We can't seem to help it. We're prone to be negative.[9]

My Story of Constant Social Media Use

The pandemic started in the spring of 2020. I focused on work. My column at Forbes.com increased in popularity, and I started a print column in *Entrepreneur* magazine and in *Popular Mechanics* around the same time. Success is not as important as fulfillment, but I kept pushing myself further. Then, in March of 2020, I took a small role at my church helping with communication strategy. I wanted to make a difference. After working only one week in an office, the pandemic forced everyone to work remotely. Meetings on Zoom became an exercise in futility because they are a poor replacement for human contact.

I started falling into a downward spiral. The church job didn't work out and some of my writing fizzled. When we experience disappointment, we have a tendency to satiate ourselves with tech. We fill the void of unproductivity with constant clicking and scrolling on websites and social media. We call scrolling through Facebook *the Facebook feed* because that's exactly what it does. It feeds us.

As Eyal explained to me and covered in his book *Indistractable*, distraction is another form of procrastination. We know we have work to do but we digress into a doom scroll. Because our work starts to slip, we then experience even more stress; we hurry up and complete more tasks, which makes us look for more quick fixes. The cycle continues. Eyal calls this *learned helplessness*.[10] I call it a vicious cycle of tech obsession.*

What if we broke the cycle? The routine at the end of this section is intended to put parameters on your social media use and help you avoid constant scrolling.

A productivity tip only carries you along for so long. You might turn off the notifications on your phone, delete a few apps for a while, or even do a social media fast. These are all good things. But they only work for a while. Let's say you turn notifications off for a month. Great! You haven't really set parameters on how you use social media. You haven't determined why you are using social media in the first place. You delayed the obsession.

In the opening chapter of this book, we learned one coping strategy—writing in a journal for seven minutes in the morning. One reason that works is because you're able to document how you are feeling. Instead of firing up your Twitter feed and checking in on the Kardashian family or reading about the latest political crisis, you deal with distraction head-on. You write down your emotions and document your feelings instead of satiating them in a way that doesn't help.

---

* You won't see the word *addiction* too often in this book. I use it sparingly on purpose. Nir Eyal, an early reader who gave me feedback, explained how addiction is a psychological condition diagnosed by professionals. In case you haven't noticed, I'm not a psychologist, I just play one on TV. Eyal likes to say we are *distracted* by technology. I prefer to say we are *obsessed*. Either way, the solution is not avoidance; it is throttled usage.

The seven-minute social media routine takes a similar approach. You set parameters for how often you use apps such as Facebook, Instagram, Twitter, and LinkedIn and decide what you want to accomplish.

There's no reason to completely abandon social media, since these apps help us connect with one another. Using them effectively means you define the purpose of the apps and learn how to control your impulses.

Measuring Your Usage

One reason we use social media so often is that we don't know how to relax and take breaks. So we get on Facebook. When we refresh the screen to see if we have more likes on a post, we experience immediate, short-term gratification with bits and bytes. The social media companies know what we're seeing has to be random, because then it's elusive and unpredictable. We keep chasing our tails, but we don't even know we have a tail.

The dangers go deeper than you might think. One example is from World War II when Adolf Hitler used similar techniques of throttling information and propaganda to foster allegiance. As John Mark Comer notes in his book *The Ruthless Elimination of Hurry*, the Nazi propaganda machine centered on wants and fears—a double-edged sword.[11] The goal was always to entice, allure, and withhold in order to maintain interest.

My son-in-law is Austrian, and he's told me stories about people who lived during that era. When prisoners escaped from concentration camps, the locals would try to ignore them and not assist their escape. Why is that? They believed in the propaganda machine of want and fear. Citizens knew the only way to buy groceries (the want) was to obey. They knew any deviation from the Nazi ideology would result in swift punishment, imprisonment, or far worse (the fear). Being caught aiding and abetting an escapee from a concentration camp was dangerous. I once visited a concentration camp in Mauthausen, Austria, and could almost hear the echoes of torture and abuse emanating from the stone walls and barred windows. Hitler focused on want and fear because that's what worked.

In recent years, teen suicide rates in the United States have risen by 150 percent according to social psychologist Jonathan Haidt. He blames social media, and the reasons seem to mirror the Hitler propaganda machine.[12]

First, the want. Teens crave the attention and how it makes them feel when they see comments and likes on social media. Adults are not immune to this. Second, the fear. In a podcast with human rights advocate Tristan Harris called *Your Undivided Attention*, Haidt explained how social media is not optional. Even if a teen decides to delete their accounts, everyone else participates. Not being on social media, especially apps like Instagram and TikTok, makes you an outcast.[13] Nielson Group estimates we check our phones about ninety-six times per day. We live on our plastic devices, doom scrolling to the bitter end.[14]

What's the answer to this dire situation? As with any obsession, it's in controlling our behavior and setting limits. The routine at the end of this section helps us do just that. Before we dive into the positive uses for social media and how to break bad habits, it's important to explain why we crave attention and why a simpler approach to social media works so well.

23

The Hyperactive Hivemind of Online Obsession

TAGGING AND LIKING on social media were not part of the original business model, as Cal Newport explains.[1] These *approval indicators* were invented after the fact. You might be surprised to learn that the "like" button was not added to Facebook until 2007, three years after the social network launched. Newport says that the iPhone was never intended to be an all-day device. When Steve Jobs announced the phone, he suggested it was more like an MP3 player that could double as a phone. Newport says social media created a frenzy of activity where we mindlessly scroll all day. It's now business as usual, funneling billions into the coffers of social media platforms.

Newport equates this perfunctory, robot-like doom scrolling with how people use a slot machine in Las Vegas. He's not kidding. The experts at social media companies studied slot machines and how they become so addictive and then modeled likes and tagging after gaming machines. You "win" when you see likes on your posts. Curiously, we barely know this is happening.

During the writing of this book, Facebook radically overhauled their interface in browsers and made it look much more appealing with bright colors and extra white space. In essence, they made it look more like a slot machine than ever before.

We are participating in constant unstructured conversations, and yet our brains were not designed to work in this haphazard way. We like to focus for short periods—let's say seven minutes at a time—and accomplish one thing. We feel productive and find meaning and purpose that way. We did *something*. The whole idea with social media, conversely, is to switch focus constantly from one thing to another. Baby pictures for a few seconds, then wedding shots, then pictures of grandma. It's a willing, constant, obsessive, and chaotic overload of our senses all day long.

Our brains need occasional periods of serenity. You can try an experiment right now to see how this works. Because visual information accounts for 30 percent of brainpower, the simple act of closing your eyes can create a sense of calm.[2] (Taking a nap is even better.) Try closing your eyes for only seven minutes, taking deep breaths as you do. You'll feel relaxed and calm because your brain had a quick respite.

〰〰〰

One thing that's critically important to understand about constant social media use is that it's a way to alleviate pain. We might not even know which pain we're trying to alleviate. It might be so deep-seated in us that we're not aware of it. Pain due to conflict at home, depression caused by working too much on meaningless tasks. We're craving false stimulation and a dopamine reward in our brains, and we don't even know why. We're seeking approval and credibility with our peers, but we have never met half of those so-called peers.

The desire to impress others is a widespread psychological pursuit known as the *sociometer*. We have social radars, and they are always on full alert.[3] Another irony is that while we try to alleviate the stress of life by using social media, we're actually *creating* more stress in our pursuit. We don't measure up to everyone else. That false sense of stress relief creates a vicious cycle as we crave more false rewards. None of it works.

Once we realize social media won't provide the answers we're looking for, the next question is, Where do we look instead?

Good question, I'm so glad you asked. I mentioned in the introduction to this book that meaning has to come first, then work. Purpose must live inside of us before we start striving after something ephemeral like workplace satisfaction. Whenever we try to find our meaning and purpose in work, we'll find that work won't quite satisfy us.

Many productivity experts who say efficiency and "being good at what you do" will lead to a better life or help you achieve more and find satisfaction are leaving out the faith component. That might sound like a bold statement, but believe me—I've tried to find meaning through my tasks. Sad to say, it doesn't work. Working hard won't make you feel better about yourself. Good productivity won't change your life or improve relationships.

What does work? First finding meaning and purpose. Then you can view work as nothing more than a means to an end because you are acting on the purpose you've already found. It changes everything about work.

Social media is merely the most obvious example of how some of us try to find meaning through clicking, liking, sharing, and commenting. Maybe if we keep scrolling through Instagram we'll relieve some anxious thoughts. There's a tendency to think we are "working" toward some goal when in fact it's an illusion of work. I like how writer Emily Gould explained that she spent years writing a novel and tricked herself into thinking she was being productive by posting on Twitter. She felt productive, but it was an escape from work.[4]

Isn't that what a lot of our quests for success look like? We strive after work and we strive after meaning, and suddenly we realize it was all a waste of time. Social media is the most obvious waste of time right now.

While many of us use social media as a salve while we're waiting in line at Starbucks, we can become much more intentional about how we use it. In the seven-minute routine at the end of this section, there's an emphasis on using social media in a much more purposeful way. Before we dive in, the next chapter explains why we keep clicking and scrolling in the first place.

24

The Relentless Pursuit of Perfection

WITH TECHNOLOGY, there is a sense that we're striving after something, and yet we don't really know what it is. Maybe it's more followers on social media or a better, faster smartphone on Amazon.

Yet when we surf the web and use Google all day, when we check Twitter, it's obvious that we are *searching*. What are we trying to find? Why do we keep looking? We click on Realtor .com and look for a new house; we switch over to Carsoup.com and "research" new cars. We read columns by authors like me. We are in constant pursuit, often for the perfect answer . . . or the perfect outfit at Old Navy.

In previous chapters, I've mentioned the scientific reasons we keep searching. But there is an even deeper spiritual reason. More than any other technological pursuit, web surfing reveals a heart condition. We dwell in the shallows of the web where it's safe and we don't have to deal with conflict or relationships or challenges of any kind. Computer scientist Jaron Lanier says we are "hooked on an elusive mirage" in that we keep striving after something that isn't real.[1] We escape the realities of life by constantly searching, which puts us in a rut. Then the *searching itself* becomes the rut. The more we keep trying to find information, the more it eludes us. Author and pastor John Ortberg summarized it clearly—we have settled for a mediocre version of faith because we're too distracted.[2]

Lanier calls this pursuit a *constant shifting of unclear rewards.* Since we don't even know what we're looking for, we won't ever find it. As I mentioned previously, this is how I'd define obsession. We don't know why we keep clicking and what the result will be. Web surfing is so mindless and never-ending that we just keep doing it.

If there was a clear goal in mind—such as buying the house or the car, using the research for a school paper, finding the recipe we need for dinner and enjoying the meal—then web surfing would not be so alluring. We'd finally stop tapping the mouse and close the lid on our laptops.

The web surfing routine at the end of this section is effective because it's designed to set parameters on web surfing and to establish clear, attainable, and achievable goals. You have only seven minutes to find your answers. You decide the intent of your surfing and click with more purpose. The social media routine also helps you sync your purpose in your career and in life, to think through why you need to spend time in the shallows.

Author John Eldredge notes that shallow pursuits such as web surfing and social media provide an endless stream of near nonsense. We click on news reports and celebrity gossip, most of it negative. We check what politicians are saying on Instagram. It's a delivery mechanism for trauma, as Eldredge explains—a constant stream of opinion, information, data, and status updates is turning us into hollow, empty shells that are being pulled toward a gravitational field that's numbing us and making us feel less human.[3] Eldredge keeps asking why that is. None of us know for sure. "My soul can't do life at the speed of a smartphone," he writes.[4] Neither can mine. Eldredge recommends simple practices such as the one-minute pause in which you simply stop, breathe, and think.

We should spend more time thinking about the transitions we need to experience in life. We don't need to click, click, click. We can pause, think, and evaluate. We can slow down. "Dry, scorched ground can't absorb the very rain it needs," Eldredge writes.[5] That's because, with web surfing and email and social media, the shallow ground is an inch deep and is not capable of sustaining us. There are billions of websites but only 168 hours in a week. Sadly, according to a Hootsuite and We Are Social report from 2018, we spend a whopping six hours and forty-two minutes online every day.[6] In case you're wondering, that's almost two full twenty-four-hour days each week.

∿∿∿

I've mentioned implementation intentions in a previous chapter—for example, the productivity technique in which you plan what you will do and then do it. Our brains are wired to complete predetermined tasks, and we are more productive when we stick to those plans.

What if we approached web surfing and social media the same way? Good plans with parameters make us more productive. What a wonderful prescription for warding off the allure of the "elusive mirage." We can stop seeking for that which cannot be found and rest in the fact that we have already found purpose, truth, meaning, and intention. We don't need to stress out about the relentless pursuit of perfection. Instead, we become content, pursuing the imperfect for a little while.

We still have time. The relentless pursuit feels familiar now and not that harmful. It's a surface level habit now, a skim just above an ocean of meaninglessness. We while away the time surfing for nothing and for no reason. Yet the illusion is alluring, and time is short. Intentionality awaits.

What if we all slowed down a little? Breathed in and out? Let the flow of intentionality prevail over the constant clicks? What if we stopped for a moment during the day, instead of clicking on every site we find, and considered why we are clicking and what we are trying to accomplish?

If only we could learn how to be more intentional in why and how we click. As Henry David Thoreau so wisely stated, "It's not enough to be busy. So are the ants. The question is: What are you busy about?"[7]

Web Surfing
ROUTINE

This routine is meant to help you set boundaries for web surfing so that you can focus on web-based tasks that help you.

▶ **BEFORE YOU START:** *Prepare*

Start by turning off all notifications on your phone and closing out of tabs you won't need in a browser. Quit apps you don't need to use. Make a show of organizing your work area; reposition your mouse and coffee cup. Remember that the routines in this book encourage focused attention for only seven minutes, so make the most of the time. As always, use a watch or a kitchen timer to track your time as you surf.

▶ **MINUTE ONE:** *Decide on the Purpose*

Before you do a web search, decide on the purpose. It might be to research the best books of the year, read about home refinancing options, or look for a recipe for dinner. Be specific. Remember to link this activity to the overall purpose you have for the day. An example of nonspecific web surfing might be looking up cute photos of puppies all day. Avoid that. For one minute during this routine, decide what your overall goal is.

▶ **MINUTE TWO:** *Perform Searches*

For the next minute, start searching. This is different from *surfing*. You are intentionally searching for web pages that help you achieve your overall purpose for being on the web in the first place. Avoid reading any of the pages you find for now. Keep track of the ones that seem helpful. Do searches for the full sixty seconds. It's okay to open new tabs or new browser windows for each search. The idea is to *search* and not to read any links.

▶ **MINUTES THREE THROUGH SIX:** *Review the Results*

Start reading the links you found, bookmark them for later research (which is not the same as surfing), or linger over a few sites that seem interesting. In this step, you are mainly reviewing the results and deciding which web pages are worth keeping for research. Close any websites that do not help you achieve the main goal.

▶ **MINUTE SEVEN:** *Summarize the Results*

Once you have organized the search results, bookmarked links, or decided how you will use the information you found, the next step is to do a summary of the results. Write down one clear statement about what you discovered when you searched and how it helped you reach your goal. Revel in the fact that you tamed your web use and made it more productive.

Social Media
ROUTINE

This routine is meant to set clear boundaries on when you check social media, how often you post, and how you can curb social media obsessions.

▶ BEFORE YOU START: *Prepare*

Decide first and foremost which social media apps and websites you need to use. It might be Facebook and Instagram only but not Twitter or LinkedIn. For business professionals, you might decide you only need to use LinkedIn. Open those apps in a browser window (because, like email, you should avoid keeping them open all day). On your phone, keep only the apps you need and remove all the others.

▶ MINUTE ONE: *Scan and Plan*

Quickly scan through any new messages but don't linger over them for too long. The idea here is to see what's new but only once and only for sixty seconds. You're mainly scrolling to see what is new and interesting but within a set window of time and only once. Be intentional with this step and avoid scrolling down, then back up, then down again.

▶ MINUTE TWO: *Like and Share*

Next, start engaging with posts as needed. Do this in a highly intentional fashion though. Most social media networks, including Facebook and Twitter, allow you to save posts or bookmark them. In Facebook, for example, go ahead and click *like* on new posts or share them but leave it at that. In Instagram, swipe down through posts quickly and like or bookmark them as needed. Don't linger too long. No need to scroll through the feed over and over. Do a quick scan, like and share, then stop.

▶ MINUTES THREE THROUGH FIVE: *Comment*

Return to the posts you bookmarked or saved and make comments or share them. At this stage in the routine, you have stopped doing any random scrolling. In fact, you only scrolled for a total of one minute and then saved or bookmarked posts. Curiously, social media companies provide these features for bookmarking because they want to provide tools for productivity. Sadly, most people don't use them. However, once you form a new habit of saving posts, you can then comment or interact with the poster (say, by starting a chat session). You are also only commenting on the most important posts.

▶ MINUTE SIX: *Post Once or Twice*

Post only once or twice in a seven-minute session. The routine for social media helps you avoid doom scrolling and spending too much time browsing feeds. Instead, when you post, you become more like a professional social media scheduler. Create the post, add an image, make it live, and move on to other tasks.

▶ MINUTE SEVEN: *Final Review*

Before moving on to more important activities, do one final pass to confirm you are not missing anything (you are probably not) and remind yourself how much time you are saving.

The Never-Ending Presentation

People don't pay attention to boring things.

—STEVE JOBS

25 ⚡

Selling an Idea in Only
Seven Minutes

I WALKED INTO a crowded ballroom at a hotel and couldn't find a seat. My name tag, clearly labeling me as a member of the press, dangled from my neck, but that didn't seem to help. The place was packed to the gills. I was at a tech conference in Austin called *South by Southwest* in 2016. A year before attending, my article about the seven-minute morning routine had created a stir and was now causing a ripple effect. Someone from the conference PR team found me. "That seven-minute morning routine really works," she whispered, confiding that she was doing "the seven" herself.

She cordoned off a small area in the back with a rope and started explaining what I was about to see. SxSW (as it's known) is a sprawling conference in a downtown area that lasts several weeks, but she said they were trying something new: a pitch event where entrepreneurs stand in front of investors, tech advocates, and the general populace (not to mention journalists) and have a set period of time to make their case.

Everything had to click, including the slideshow, the music, the explanations, and the jokes. The conference planned to award several start-ups with a small investment to help them kick-start their idea.

As I settled in for the presentations, the PR contact started smiling. "So guess how long they have?" she asked in a friendly way. I had no idea. I'd assumed most pitch events, like those I'd seen at other conferences and at *Inc.* events in the past, were about ten to fifteen minutes. She rolled her eyes. "We gave them seven minutes, of course!" I was surprised by that and yet also knew this time frame is based on sustained attention span. I wasn't about to take credit; it was merely a happy coincidence.*

To this day, I remember the first pitch. An entrepreneur walked to the front of the room and told a story about his kids. With each bullet point, he showed a brightly colored image or a graph. The presentation was more like an accent to what he was saying, and he followed the first rule of all presentations: never just repeat what is on the screen. His app helps you keep track of screen time for your kids. I was sold. I later found out, so were the conference organizers. He not only won the pitch event, but his company also went on to become a viable market player.

∿∿∿

One collective "bad habit" in business, classrooms, tech conferences, churches, and even the Vegan Baking Club meetup is to think a presentation should run for forty-five minutes or longer. We tend to fill a time slot with too much information, thinking that's what helps people connect with an idea. It doesn't. The same principles you use for the morning routine and to check

* And here is another one. An early reader of this book, a college professor, mentioned the Pecha Kucha technique for giving presentations. You use twenty slides and talk about each one for twenty seconds. Math wizards will know that totals about seven minutes per presentation. "It's abundantly clear who understands the material and who doesn't," he says. "It doesn't advantage those who have the gift of gab over those who don't."

your email apply to giving a presentation. Besides, people only *really* pay attention for the first seven minutes.

A few caveats to mention here. The presentation routine at the end of this section is meant for situations when you are selling an idea, giving a short talk to a board of directors, or have a limited time frame.

It's not meant to replace a presentation during a college course, as an example. If you are a student (or the professor) you might need to share thirty or forty slides as part of an assignment. If you are training employees at work on the benefits package to select for health insurance, this routine is not meant for you. (Although many of the principles still apply.)

The presentation routine works for many situations where you have a captive audience and need to cover a lot of ground in a short period. As you'll see in the routine described in this section, the basic idea is to wow them with a catchy opening story, summarize what you will say quickly, give them the "meat" of the presentation, remind them again about your main points, then close with a quick summary and call to action.

∿∿

This section offers practical tips on how to give a presentation in seven minutes. Surprisingly, in researching this book, the topic of engaging a crowd, holding their attention, and giving them an action step at the end is not well-documented—at least in terms of scientific studies and surveys to find out what works best based on profiling a large audience.

What you will find are pseudoscience books that talk about the sales process as though you're luring mice through a maze. We'll skip that type of pontificating, mostly because those books seem like a way to build the confidence of the salesperson rather than increase sales.

What makes a presentation capture the crowd? There is one person we can herald as the ultimate example of what works: Steve Jobs.

∿∿∿

Long before I attended SxSW in Austin in 2016, and even before I worked as a journalist and columnist starting in 2001, I led a large information design practice at a retail giant based in the Minneapolis area. (It wasn't Circuit City, so you can likely guess which one.) My team designed websites, wrote documentation, and built help systems used by over fifty thousand employees. Small claim to fame here: one app we developed for the point-of-sale (POS) system at the time included a user interface the clerks used for many years; I made the little POS buttons myself.

Because graphic design was central to our work, the company sent me to the Macworld conference in Boston every year. Later, Apple would relocate the conference to San Francisco, and I kept attending. It morphed into what we know today: a glitzy Apple-only event to announce new devices.

We were a captive audience, held "captive" by the fact that we had limited options. Computers were not that powerful back then, the web barely even existed, and Google was only a figment of the imagination of two Stanford college grads named Sergey Brin and Larry Page. If you are doing the math, you may have figured out the year was 1997. Just three years earlier, I had attended Macworld in Boston and witnessed Stephen Hawking using a speech synthesizer to wow a small crowd at the Park Plaza hotel.

This year, another luminary walked onto the stage.

He was wearing a white shirt with a black vest.

∿∿∿

Steve Jobs had rejoined Apple as CEO in 1997, but back then he was known more for his work running Pixar than anything else. No iPhone, no iPad, and no deification as the smartest tech wizard ever. I was in the crowd, and I was stunned. I pulled out a journal and started writing down not only what he said but also *how he said it*. His first slides were about negative press. He made a few jokes—for example, "Apple is executing wonderfully . . . on many of the wrong things."* He then gave an engaging presentation about how Apple would reemerge as a monolith of tech.[1]

That seemed to work out as planned, right? By the time Jobs died in 2011 after a long battle with pancreatic cancer, the company reached a market capitalization of over $350 billion.[2] Today, it's $2 trillion.[3]

Even though the entire presentation was about thirty minutes long, here's an interesting discovery: his opening remarks lasted about seven minutes. Even back then, Jobs knew he would only have a captive audience for a short segment of time. After seven minutes, he switched over to several vignettes and random segues to break up the monotony. If you watch the keynote on YouTube, he covers the salient points in the first seven minutes. The rest seems like filler, even for a luminary like Jobs.†

He seemed aware of the limited window of time that people would listen to his words of advice and explanation. It worked. Jobs announced a partnership with Microsoft that year, impressed the crowd (including me), and went on to usher Apple into an age of total domination. It's not hard to make the case that it all started with that Macworld talk.

〰〰

Most of us won't lead a $2 trillion company. I've done countless presentations in the last few years, and the one constant in all of them is that you have seven minutes to make a good impression. You can go much longer than that, but the rule of thumb is that you have to make the most of the first few minutes.

As we've covered, sustained attention is based on science. In the next chapter, let's take a closer look at how that helps you.

* That's a good summary of how many of us work.

† Even in later years, Jobs delivered his best material in the first seven minutes. He did often end a presentation with "one more thing" that (you guessed it) also lasted about seven minutes. In between? Filler.

26

How Sustained Attention Span Works

SCIENTISTS TELL US we can focus our attention for about seven minutes. Having the routines in this book last seven minutes helps you implement them easily. Sadly, presentations in the real world sometimes last far longer than seven minutes.

The seven-minute presentation routine described later in this section helps place boundaries on the length. You'll learn how to pack in all the critical details, the ones that will "sell" your idea more than others'.

Writing an article is a distant cousin to *giving a presentation*. When writing an article, you chisel away the fat, hone your skills, and sculpt an award-worthy piece. When giving a presentation, you have seven minutes to click through slides or tell a story. With the self-imposed time restraint, you'll become a whiz at organizing your thoughts and wowing the crowd. As author Carmine Gallo has noted, people stop paying attention to you after ten minutes anyway.[1] There's nothing we can do about that.

What we can do is fill the time we have more intentionally. You can customize for your audience like Steve Jobs at Macworld and set time limits or even borrow from the TED talk format (which varies in length from about three to no more than eighteen minutes). So how do you do that in practical terms? What is the secret? One man from history knew the answer.

〜〜〜

Dale Carnegie was a failed actor living in New York in 1912. He worked as a salesman for the automaker Packard and could barely afford rent. Around this time, though living in abject poverty, he enrolled in a prestigious course at the American Academy of Dramatic Arts that emphasized an authentic delivery style. (Later he would write his famous book *How to Win Friends and Influence People*.)

Taking what he had learned about public speaking and theatrics to heart, Carnegie decided to quit his sales job and offer a course at the local YMCA. At first, his pay was a respectable two dollars per class (or about fifty dollars today); his lectures were highly choreographed to appear genuine. He didn't use the more common approach of the day of making dramatic gestures and posing like a statue with something important to say. He moved around the stage and spoke as though he was your close friend. If that sounds a bit like Steve Jobs, it's probably no accident.

One night, he finished a talk too early after making his usual remarks. (So much for being highly choreographed.) He had to improvise, but he sensed the crowd was a bit restless. He decided to try something new.

"Think of something that makes you angry," he asked. Suddenly everyone started paying attention as multiple participants shared their feelings. Carnegie tapped into something profound. He decided to engage with them in an honest and open way, to connect over a shared reality.

From that moment on, Carnegie would always make a similar homespun connection and avoid making it seem as if he was unapproachable and remote. It's a principle the Dale Carnegie

Institute still espouses when they use the tagline "transformation begins from within," which hints at honesty and authenticity in any presentation or lecture.[2] It has been weaved into presentations Steve Jobs gave and is the de facto approach in almost every TED Talk. It's also the best way to give a presentation today.

Earlier in this book, I mentioned James Veitch. In his famous TED Talk about spam, he starts out by saying, "A few years ago, I got one of those spam emails."[3] I call that *instant empathy*. He has you in his grasp. We listen because we can relate to that opening line. Spam is infuriating! We hate spam, so we lean forward and listen intently.

Ever notice how the words *intent* and *intentional* are closely linked? That's no accident. Both words mean *clearly formulated*.

By having an intentional approach, you are acting with intent and helping people lean into what you are about to say. Since you have their attention for only seven minutes, no matter how long you actually speak, being intentional makes sense. Before Carnegie died in 1955, about 450,000 people had attended one of his courses. Around 30 million people bought his book. Everyone knows his name.

〰〰

So here's the important question to answer in this section: Why are most presentations so *unintentional*? We're so bored by most lectures we would rather watch someone vacuum an airplane.

I blame Microsoft PowerPoint. Released back in 1987 while I was still in college, the app has been the scourge of all business meetings ever since. We let the slides dazzle and entertain, even though most of them do not have any dazzle or entertainment value. Mainly, they include boring two-color charts and a couple of cartoons. Amazon actually bans the app.[4]

Business executive Robert Pozen recounts a story of a famous PowerPoint slide used during the war in Afghanistan. You can find it on Google by searching for "Afghan War PowerPoint" and gaze at the jaw-dropping complexity. As General Stanley McChrystal said at the time, "When we understand that slide, we'll have won the war."[5]

The problem is that PowerPoint is a poor substitute for starting out with a catchy story at the beginning of your sales pitch or business meeting. It's less effective than relaying specific examples and asking for a response from the attenders, as outlined in the presentation routine.

Even showing a video doesn't quite work these days. People can pull out their phones and watch something far more interesting on YouTube.

I experienced "the PowerPoint problem" once when I was mentoring college students. I had not followed my own advice and started a new presentation about social media trends without preparing first. They could tell I was winging it. After speaking for a few minutes about the dangers of Twitter trolls, much of the material invented on the spot off the top of my head (which is never a good source), I could tell I was losing these Gen Z students, most of them around twenty years old. They know when you are spitballing. I decided to wrap up the ad hoc presentation early and switched to a brainstorming session.

I had learned my lesson. By the next time I met with them, I had done my homework. The students attended a local Bible college in my area, and I knew I had to present salient facts in a short amount of time. The Gen Z attention span is roughly eight seconds, according to a study by the IBM Institute for Business Value.[6] (Fun fact: the millennial attention span lasts twelve seconds according to the same study.) If attention span lasts eight seconds and sustained attention span—meaning, when we focus more intently—lasts seven minutes, every second counts. So does every minute.

In the presentation routine, you'll learn to move quickly from opening statement to salient points to the closing summary and call to action. Make it quick! I often follow my own advice when I'm pitching editors on an article idea. Remember that no presentation should rely on the slides. Grab their attention and hang on for the ride. Fill in the details. Then be ready to instill action and response at the end, as we'll cover in the next chapter.

27

Closing the Deal in Your Presentation

Brittany Thoms strode on stage at the Classic Center in Athens, Georgia, one day in 2020. The small business owner runs a PR agency that represents major companies like Airstream and has helped promote events such as Passion Conferences and Catalyst. Even though the Stronger Branding conference had gone virtual during the pandemic, there were still dozens of attenders in person (all socially distanced, of course) and a large livestream audience.

She had one shot to impress them. She followed a presentation technique espoused by Dr. Tim Elmore, an author and speaker who writes frequently about connecting with younger generations. She had learned to engage with an audience right away, so she started with a slide with the single word *lie* in large, bold print. She wanted to speak about truth in advertising and to connect that to examples of good branding.

Thoms has spoken at major events before. At her church in Atlanta, she's given presentations to sixty thousand people. On this day, she had a formula for success. After showing the slide with the word *lie*, she showed slides with the words *truth* and *trust*. Thoms has a spirited delivery style. She could read her grocery list, and it would sound interesting. But as a business owner, her goal was to explain why branding and marketing are about relaying the truth about a company in a clear and understandable way.

She chose Disney World as a good example. Her slides included details about how the theme park does not sell gum (you will never see a sticky mess on a ride or on your shoe), there are trash cans every fifty feet, and none of the staff will ever say the words *I don't know* to a guest. She rattled through a few more slides and, in her call to action, made the point that her agency assists only brands they would use themselves.

Thoms says she yearns to "do things that make her scared," and for many of us, giving presentations puts the fear of the Lord in our souls. In your lifetime, you might give thousands of presentations if you work in business or sales. Thoms runs an agency with twenty-four employees and has major clients in part because she communicates effectively.[1] "Effectiveness is doing the right things," author Peter Drucker stated.[2]

When we give effective presentations, we convey purpose and meaning in a way that leads to results. Author Nancy Duarte said in her famous TED Talk about presentations in 2011: "A presentation has the power to change the world if it conveys an idea effectively."[3]

Yet as Duarte explains, no one wants to settle for mere communication. We want *action*. That means "closing the deal" to encourage actual response as opposed to simply nodding in agreement. As Thoms explained to me, her goal that day was to create excitement about branding, to move people from one state of thought to another—to transform their thinking.

⌁

Closing the deal does not mean becoming rich, gaining more customers for your widget company, or looking smart. It's something more important. I'm talking about the listener realizing your presentation met their needs and was worth the time investment. All seven minutes of it! I believe Dale Carnegie was correct: people know when you are being authentic. Every presentation should be highly choreographed and tuned for response.

You might call this concept *knowing your audience*.* If what you have to offer has any hope of not falling on deaf ears, it might be best to find out who is in the crowd and if they will be willing to accept what you say.

The presentation routine we'll cover next is meant to attune attention—to start with an engaging opening summary, to present the most critical facts quickly in an engaging way, and to close with a summary that leads to a response. Let's dive into how this routine can help you communicate ideas in a way that's effective, translates easily, and leads to authentic results.

---

* Knowing your audience reveals a great deal of confidence and empathy. What you have to say is worth their time, and you care how much time that requires.

Presentation
ROUTINE

This routine is meant to help you run a smooth (and short) presentation. Cover the most important topics and leave room at the end (after the first seven minutes) for discussion or more detail.

▶ BEFORE YOU START: *Prepare*

Decide what your presentation will be about before ever starting this routine. Keep a stopwatch or a kitchen timer handy to hone your presentation to seven minutes.

▶ MINUTE ONE: *Get Their Attention*

Start the presentation with a bang. Show a picture of your kids, for example. Spark interest and give people the time they need to adjust to your delivery style, the room where you are standing, or even the lighting. It helps prepare them for the topic. Use the first minute to garner trust as well. Make sure your attention-grabbing technique flows into the real topic. Remember, you only have one minute to make an impact.

▶ MINUTE TWO: *Summarize the Topic Quickly*

Spend about one minute summarizing the topic. Make it quick! Tell them what to expect. Make sure you make the most of the attention you grabbed at the outset. Explain in one sentence what you are covering in your presentation—what you're selling, suggesting, explaining, or offering. Be succinct and clear. If you can't summarize the talk in one clear statement, keep revising until you can. Avoid being too elaborate at this stage.

▶ **MINUTES THREE THROUGH SIX:** *Give the Presentation*

You've grabbed their attention and summarized the talk. Great! Now spend the bulk of the presentation giving them the meat. Cover the main bullet points of your presentation but avoid reading your slides. Remember that you are making the most of the seven minutes you have and the seven minutes the audience is giving you. Cover your main points in four minutes, breezing through them clearly and smoothly. Include engaging stats and surveys, visuals, and anecdotes. Keep it tidy, trim, and upbeat.

▶ **MINUTE SEVEN:** *Summarize It Again*

You are six minutes into the presentation and, even if you are the most skilled communicator on the planet, you only have one minute left before people start thinking about lunch. Use the last minute to do a quick recap of the presentation. Close with a quick anecdote or summary statement so the last thing you say in a presentation is also the most important thing they remember. And make sure you give them a call to action (how to respond).

Boring Old Meetings

The secret of being boring is to say everything.

—VOLTAIRE

28

Why the Best Meetings Are Short

IMAGINE A SIT-DOWN MEETING with the biblical figure Noah. There's not a cloud in the sky. You see a large wooden table with a bowl of fruit in the center. Noah is holding a wooden staff, has a long beard, and looks a bit like Russell Crowe. He assembles the team, consisting mostly of family members and perhaps a few confused onlookers.

"So I want to build an ark," he explains to a chorus of groans and eye rolls, some of them from his wife and kids.

The initial reaction seems a bit hostile. "What's an ark?" someone asks from the back. It's a serious question many attendees have, especially those who feel as if they're being enlisted to help build one.

You're at the meeting, watching this all unfold. It's a bit puzzling. You glance over at a zebra grazing in a field. Actually, you notice two zebras, which seems odd. Noah yammers on about a flood and the moral depravity of, well . . . anyone not at the meeting it seems. It's a bit cray cray, but Russell Crowe seems to know what he's talking about. He has *details*. We're talking exact measurements and specific plans. The size of this thing! Bigger than a Costco. The zebras start inching closer.

In all seriousness, this meeting never happened. (Or maybe it did?) We do know from Genesis 6:22 that "Noah did everything just as God commanded him." By the next chapter in Genesis, he was on the ark with his family.

Blink and you might miss it.

I like to think Noah was incredibly efficient and communicated clearly to everyone involved, because if he dawdled, the rains would come and they would not survive. He had vision; he had purpose. Let's be honest: if he did have a meeting with his sons and their wives to explain what was about to happen, those meetings were short, to the point, and a little urgent.

〰〰〰

I'm always amazed when people present a vision in a way that seems not only *possible* but also *plausible*. They have specific details to share, not just a poorly formed idea and a lot of spare time (which will waste *your* time). One person is going to launch a floating arboretum powered by nuclear fission and explains how to do that; another is going to send people to the moon and back and explains it in a way that seems as simple as a trip to the grocery store.

The best meetings are like that. As the entrepreneur Arianna Huffington said, "If we have a clear agenda in advance and we are fully present and fully contributing, the meetings do go much faster."[1]

Picture an Elon Musk–like figure at the head of the table presenting a clear and compelling argument about a mission to Mars. You take it all in and nod in agreement. It's short and to the point. While some meetings are like watching dueling ostriches peck at each other for an hour, others feel far more intentional. There's a goal to the meeting, and it's to present a vision to help everyone make a decision. Also, they are short. The best meetings seem to go as smooth as butter.

∿

I prefer meetings that run like a football huddle. Call the play, provide the details, give the snap count, and then execute.

In this book, I've advocated for slowing down on most of our tasks, but not when it comes to meetings. I like meetings that pop with intentional purpose. Meetings ought to be more like a huddle: present the vision, share the details, make a critical decision, and move on.

Being more efficient with our time during meetings frees us up to focus on other meaningful tasks. Poorly run, time-consuming, and inefficient meetings are a collective bad habit. There is no vision during those meetings, only stale donuts and mindless banter.

I wish more of us running meetings would listen to the entrepreneur Gary Vaynerchuk who said that none of us will ever find more time.[2] Comedian Dave Barry once said, "If you had to identify, in one word, the reason why the human race has not achieved, and never will achieve, its full potential, that word would be 'meetings.'"[3]

Meetings are boring and unproductive when they lack vision and take too long.

Vision involves two components: *where you plan to go* and *how you plan to get there*. Those who are terrible at vision casting might set an admirable goal for a meeting but not explain how to get there. At any meeting, it's important to explain the purpose and vision and then provide the details on what is at stake and what needs to happen. Meetings help us to quickly solidify a vision within a group. As author Chris Hodges has noted, your vision is likely too big to implement by yourself.[4]

Peter Drucker once wrote, "Don't tell me you had a wonderful meeting with me. Tell me what you are going to do on Monday that's different."[5] My view is that all huddles—those that follow the seven-minute meeting routine at the end of this section—should use a similar approach: emphasize what needs to be done outside of the meeting, present the important details with a call to action, then *end*.

Before we dive into the best way to conduct meetings, let's address the elephant in the room. You're probably wondering how any meeting could last seven minutes. You might run a status meeting at work that lasts two hours! I feel your pain. It's easy to write in a journal for seven minutes, and a seven-minute presentation to pitch an idea makes sense, especially if you have any familiarity with the drudgery of PowerPoint.

But meetings are different. They are robust. They are long. They are boring. You could argue they are prime candidates for radical retooling.

My idea is to turn more meetings into huddles meant for making quick decisions. It means eliminating most meetings that look like the following:

Endless discussions of topics with no decisions
Status meetings that never talk about the status of anything
Get-to-know-you meetings that aren't that effective
The boss telling everyone bad jokes
Meetings where everyone is on their phone anyway
Arguments based on your cachet at the company, not the
   actual topic

Turning meetings into huddles to make decisions will save about fifty-three minutes per meeting. Why? You don't need to meet for an hour—only seven minutes. You can use that extra time for research, analyzing market trends, building rapport in an ad hoc setting, or doing other work.* You're relocating

---

* But definitely not doom scrolling at ESPN.com the rest of the day.

the meeting to another venue—say, a task management app like Trello or a collaborative chat tool like Slack or Microsoft Teams.

In this section, we'll redefine the purpose of most meetings and off-load the heavy lifting. I've had seven-minute huddles that were far more valuable than any hour-long (or daylong) meetings.

∿∿∿

Rahul Vohra, CEO and founder of the Superhuman app, once told me about the interesting way he runs meetings.[6] First, they are extremely short. No one brings up a topic unless they have shared the idea the day before and everyone has read it and commented on it. Most meetings are early in the week so that people have time throughout the week to implement the decisions made.

There are two types of decisions his team makes at meetings. One is called a *reversible decision*, something that's not so earth-shattering that it will disrupt their business. Vohra says he never makes the final call on reversible decisions and allows team members to remind him of that. Only other people can make final decisions that are reversible.

Irreversible decisions, on the other hand, are those that make a huge impact. An example Vohra gave is when the team is thinking about choosing an investor in his start-up. In that case, he always makes the final call. He says every start-up knows you can't "divorce" your investors. That means, once you choose one, you are obligated to make it work.

His team also has a rule that no topic on the table can be discussed for more than five minutes. For our purposes, the entire meeting routine lasts seven minutes, but remember these huddles are not for every purpose at every company. You can't do a human resources training meeting in seven minutes, no matter how awesome that sounds.

There is a specific criterion that must be met in order to follow the seven-minute meeting routine. The meeting must involve a decision that has already been discussed at length and is meant for making final decisions. Before you have a seven-minute "decision huddle," discuss all the variables in smaller groups, by phone, or using other methods. The seven-minute meeting is designed to form a new habit that fosters more intentionality and efficiency at all meetings, avoids belaboring topics, and encourages brainstorming elsewhere.

∿∿∿

Most of us have some attention problems. Meetings often put that to a test, as you've likely witnessed. A fun game to play at a meeting is to set a timer and see how long it takes for someone to pull out their phone. I blame an overload of information. Economist Herbert Simon once eloquently said that we "need to allocate that attention efficiently among the overabundance of information sources that might consume it."[7]

Author Robert Pozen has written about how corporate meetings are often inefficient and even unnecessary. They lack meaning and purpose, they occur too often, and they last too long. Meetings are not the best way to encourage interpersonal relationships. They often result in endless debates that do not help anyone finish their work.[8]

Some companies have addressed the incredible inefficiency of most meetings by doing stand-ups (quick meetings to summarize important tasks) and even walking meetings, the kind Steve Jobs used to hold with employees[9] (which have fallen out of favor in recent years and during the pandemic).

Unfortunately, many of these techniques do not address the underlying problem: we do not pay attention at meetings, even when walking or standing in a group. Researchers even back in the 1970s knew that. A study profiling college students found that participants stopped listening after only ten minutes into a lecture. Ten minutes! This was before people had social media accounts, cell phones, tablets, laptops, and YouTube.[10]

Surely, there must be a better way to make decisions as a group than to put twenty to thirty people in a room for an hour. In the next chapter, I'll make the case that meetings should be mostly geared for decision-making.

29

Resolve Problems in Seven Minutes

I **FIRST STARTED** holding seven-minute meetings when I helped a local college with marketing and social media strategy. It was 2016, and I realized there was an opportunity to include students in the process.

I created a digital marketing team to help schedule social media posts, write articles, take photos at events, and make videos. It was incredibly successful. The social media platforms grew from a few hundred to several thousand followers in three years—a 750 percent growth rate.

One key to success was that we made decisions quickly.

The students didn't know this at the time—although some of them have realized it since then—but it was common for me to gather a small group of no more than seven or eight workers, many of them volunteers and interns, and present an idea about a new strategy or project. Time was of the essence. For one thing, I wasn't there throughout the week for the first few years. When I started in 2016, I wasn't even living in the same town.

By 2017, with about thirty students involved, I would hold impromptu meetings in a large room the college dedicated to our digital marketing efforts. In many cases, after vision casting for a minute or two, we'd then discuss the best avenue to complete our objectives. Here's just one example among literally hundreds over a four-year period. Early on, we thought about how our social media could benefit from having influencers who shared and liked the articles. If we could find influencers with large numbers of Twitter followers, for instance, that could lead to higher awareness for the college. That became a good vision statement as it was easy to explain in about one or two minutes. Next, we threw out ideas for how to find influencers.

At our meetings, we focused on key decisions. We weren't trying to brainstorm. Instead, we set out a clear goal as a team and then looked at a specific objective and tactics and considered a small handful of options. We decided to research alumni with a large following on social media and email them to ask if they would become part of an influencer network. Bingo! The group briefly discussed how this would work, but all the actual work occurred outside of the meeting. So did the brainstorming. And the discussion about the budget.

In short, the meeting wasn't where we had the discussion or did the actual work. We assigned the work on a collaborative messaging app like Slack and avoided endless chatter and brainstorming sessions. Later, if we needed to hold more discussions, we did that in smaller groups on the spur of the moment and wouldn't even call it a meeting.

∿∿∿

This is radical stuff if you have ever been to a meeting. Productivity with purpose means constant examination. It means we cut out the fluff.

Most meetings are a bad habit today because they are mostly fluff. The way to improve meetings is to keep them short, focused, and regimented.

Why is that important? Jordan Raynor wrote about the problem of distraction and letting too many priorities pull us in too many directions. *Master of One: Find and Focus on the Work You Were Created to Do* is a masterful explanation of why it's not possible to "do it all" in a way that's glorifying to God and matches up with our higher calling.

He once told me how we're all stuck in a swamp trying to make good decisions. Some of us say "we're swamped" with work, but in reality, *the swamp is our competing priorities*. I'm not sure how you would drain that swamp, but it's probably best not to ever be in one.

This might seem counterintuitive, but author Robert Pozen advises that we all decline more meetings than we accept on a regular basis, depending on your situation.[1]

The truth is all of us could stand to take a hard look at whether our meetings are necessary or could be accomplished using other communication channels. Meanwhile, more efficient meetings need an entirely new recipe for success, one that—as we'll see in the next chapter—is highly focused.

30

How to Focus Your Meetings and Your Time

HERE'S AN INTERESTING thought experiment.

Imagine for a moment you are Sir Isaac Newton, the man who discovered the universal law of gravity. Feel free to picture that iconic tree and the apple that hits him on the head. Think about a bright fall day, the loud clunk on his noggin, and the resulting bruise. Ouch!

Now, if you were in that situation and were in a highly contemplative mood like the protagonist in our thought experiment, you would have already pondered universal gravity. It would already have hit you like a ton of bricks. Why is that? Because it would have already been on your mind.

Of course, some of the facts about Isaac Newton are not quite accurate. An apple never really fell on his head.[1] That fable entered the public lexicon because it artfully simplifies how a brilliant man discovered gravity. What they didn't tell you in school is that *he had been thinking about gravity for many years*. Objects of different size are drawn to each other—in this case, an apple is drawn to the planet. When asked how he discovered the law of gravity, Newton replied, "By thinking about it continually."[2]

Scientists are convinced this ability is due to something called *hyperfocus*—that is, an ability to block out all other distractions and stay centered on one thought. The fact that we can focus on one idea at a time means we are not thinking about breakfast, what we want to post on Instagram, and why one of our kids isn't doing so well in school at the same time.

Our brains are wired to laser focus on one topic at a time. They were not designed to switch constantly from one app to another or to multitask from one business document to another. We prefer *focus*.

As a writer, I've zeroed in on a few key areas such as productivity, technology, leadership, and mentoring. Seth Godin, the marketing genius, has said that every company needs to find their niche—an area of extreme focus. By finding differentiators, he says, you can then create marketing plans and attract customers.[3]

Too many firms try to go broad and wide to draw in as many new customers as possible, but Godin says this is a recipe for disaster. Trying to attract every type of customer means you won't attract any.

A narrow gate draws more attention.

What's happening when we focus? For starters, it's a *wonder*. The human brain is unique in that it can even do that. We turn our attention to a political topic or a plate of food or a significant other. When we wonder about something or someone, we're automatically tuning everything else out.

If our brains did not have an ability to focus, we'd be constantly refocusing every minute of the day. We would not be able to work on spreadsheets or build bridges or make a raspberry pie. That's why, to be efficient, it's important to focus continually.

Meetings are one glaring example of how a lack of focus leads to unproductivity. It doesn't have to be that way. Time is precious, and it can be optimized. In fact, now is a good time to wrap things up.

Meeting
ROUTINE

What some people might call a *huddle* is essentially the same as the seven-minute meeting. You are gathering people together to follow a strict seven-minute agenda.

▶ BEFORE YOU START: *Prepare*

Plan what you will say and what decision you want to make during the seven-minute meeting routine. Create an exact agenda for the seven minutes that accounts for every minute as outlined below. Before the huddle, create and distribute an agenda so the attenders know what to expect—and how long you will meet.

▶ MINUTE ONE: *Announce Your Intentions*

Start by announcing how quickly the meeting will run. That will go over quite nicely. State the decision you are seeking to make—for example, to decide on the name of a new marketing campaign or to choose someone to lead a company event. Explain the decision you want and the purpose of the meeting in only one minute. Don't go too long or overexplain the purpose.

▶ MINUTES TWO THROUGH FIVE: *Cover the Basic Options*

Because this is a short huddle meant to make a decision on one topic as a group, review the basic findings and information you already distributed in order to make the decision. You have only four minutes, so quickly explain the choices. If you're meeting to decide on someone to lead a new sales initiative, list the candidates and their qualifications. If you're deciding on food for an after-work party, explain the choices to the group.

▶ MINUTE SIX: *Raise Any Concerns*

After covering the basic options available to the group, which you listed in the agenda and distributed beforehand (so they had a chance to think about them), now give everyone a chance to raise any concerns or ask questions. Since the agenda is clear, the group knows this part of the huddle only lasts a minute.

▶ MINUTE SEVEN: *Make the Decision*

This quick and fast-paced huddle is meant to bring a small group together and to provide a forum for having a quick discussion and making a decision. Don't linger. In the final minute, after you have presented the options and allowed a brief period to state any concerns, make a decision as a group. Schedule any follow-up brainstorming and action items as needed.

Epilogue

Ending on a Good Minute

IF YOU FEEL that there's a constant battle for your attention, you are not alone. We're dancing to the tune of a hundred emails and texts serenading us all day long. Our social media feeds are on a feeding frenzy; email chains become jail sentences. To stay productive, some of us resort to extreme measures such as deleting our Facebook accounts . . . or moving to a deserted island.

It doesn't have to be that way.

Productivity with purpose is all about following repeatable routines with clear intentions. What you focus on will become your greatest area of success, as I've noted in this book. With intentionality comes a wonderful benefit: a sense of purpose and peace, knowing you're working toward the right goals.

You've learned to fight against distraction using the routines in this book, and you've come a long way. My encouragement now is simple: stick with the plan. Distractions may still derail you at times (after all, those baby photos on Facebook are adorable). You'll lose a few productivity battles here and there. But cherish those moments when you finish your morning routine or when you breeze through your emails in only seven minutes.

There's something incredibly satisfying about those times when you finish a routine and close the cover of your journal or quit an email app, when you finally close the lid of your laptop for the day. You stand up and push your chair back with a smile; you made serious progress.

I'm right there with you. The lesson I've learned this past year, writing this book mostly during a pandemic and practicing my own routines, is this: stress happens. The question is not whether we should avoid stress and stay comfortable. The question is, How will we respond to the stress?

The routines in this book are designed to help you thrive in your productivity—not for a few months and a few short-term gains but rather as a lifelong, radical shift in how you approach work in the first place. It means setting aside your bad habits and learning new routines that will reset your entire outlook.

As we've seen, being intentional about productivity, slowing down and thinking about what you're doing and why, can lead to more purpose and meaning. You can work hard on the right tasks as opposed to working fast on the wrong ones. That's productivity with purpose.

Writing in a journal and recording the hope moments in your life; planning your day and working on the most important tasks; casting aside the tasks that are not essential; looking back on your day with an intentional, honest perspective; breaking bad habits such as social media obsession and web surfing; and resisting never-ending presentations and unproductive meetings—you've done it all!

In the end, my prayer for you is that the routines in this book will help you throughout your entire life and that you'll come to see productivity as more than something you read about in a book. My hope is that it defines who you are.

I'm here to help. Visit my website sevenminutesolution.com to find out how to keep fighting the battle of distraction and to learn new productivity techniques or to drop me a line and say hello. I promise to respond . . . eventually.

Notes

Introduction

1. Greg McKeown, *Essentialism: The Disciplined Pursuit of Less* (New York: Random House, 2014), 207–8.

2. Maria Popova, "William James on the Psychology of Habit," BrainPickings, September 25, 2012, https://www.brainpickings.org/2012/09/25/william-james-on-habit.

3. Ryan Holiday, *Stillness Is the Key* (London: Portfolio, 2019), 200.

4. Diane M. Bunce, Elizabeth A. Flens, and Kelly Y. Neiles, "How Long Can Students Pay Attention in Class? A Study of Student Attention Decline Using Clickers," *Journal of Chemical Education* 87, no. 12 (October 22, 2010): 1838–43, https://doi.org/10.1021/ed100409p.

5. John Brandon, "Is Google Doing Enough to Protect Kids from Disturbing YouTube Videos?," Fox News, September 9, 2019, https://www.foxnews.com/tech/google-kids-disturbing-youtube-videos.

6. John Brandon, "Crazy Passion," *Christianity Today*, October 16, 2009, https://www.christianitytoday.com/ct/2009/october/30.42.html.

7. John Brandon, "5 Signs Your Employees Are about to Turn against You," *Inc.*, December 21, 2015, https://www.inc.com/john-brandon/5-signs-your-employees-are-about-to-revolt-against-you.html.

8. John Brandon, "Oaks of Righteousness," Alliance, accessed April 12, 2021, https://www.cmalliance.org/alife/oaks-of-righteousness/.

9. Ann Brown, "How Many Breaths Do You Take Each Day?," *EPA Blog*, April 28, 2014, https://blog.epa.gov/2014/04/28/how-many-breaths-do-you-take-each-day/.

10. Ryder Carroll, "How to Declutter Your Mind—Keep a Journal," YouTube video, 12:50, posted by "Tedx Talks," January 20, 2017, https://www.youtube.com/watch?v=ym6OYelD5fA. Carroll said 500,000 but he obviously meant 50,000; see Ryder Carroll, "The Mental Inventory," Bullet Journal, accessed April 12, 2021, https://bulletjournal.com/blogs/bulletjournalist/mental-inventory.

11. Mark Buchanan, phone interview with author, August 12, 2020, transcript and audio recording available.

12. Timothy Keller, *Every Good Endeavor: Connecting Your Work to God's Work* (New York: Penguin, 2014), 67.

13. John Brandon, "This 7-Minute Morning Routine Will Change Your (Work) Life," *Inc.*, May 19, 2015, https://www.inc.com/john-brandon/this-7-minute -morning-routine-will-change-your-work-life.html.

Chapter 1 Define What Is Meaningful

1. Gary Keller and Jay Papasan, *The ONE Thing: The Surprisingly Simple Truth Behind Extraordinary Results* (Austin: Bard Press, 2014), 187.

2. Keller and Papasan, *The ONE Thing*, 187.

Chapter 2 You're Smarter in the Morning

1. The Immanuel Kant story is an amalgamation of several facts from multiple sources: Mason Currey, Daily Rituals: How Artists Work (New York: Knopf, 2013), 273, EPUB; Mark Manson, "The One Rule for Life," Mark Manson, accessed August 21, 2021, https://markmanson.net/the-one-rule-for-life; "A Philosophy of Walking: Thoreau, Nietzsche and Kant on Walking," *Farnam Street* (blog), accessed August 21, 2021, https://fs.blog/2014/05/a-philosophy-of -walking; "The Daily Habits of Highly Productive Philosophers: Nietzsche, Marx & Immanuel Kant," Open Culture, October 3, 2013, https://www.openculture .com/2013/10/the-daily-habits-of-highly-productive-philosophers.html; Drake Baer, "The Workday Secrets Of The World's Most Productive Philosophers," Fast Company, October 9, 2013, https://www.fastcompany.com/3019654/the -workday-secrets-of-the-worlds-most-productive-philosophers; Mark Manson, "How To Be More Productive by Working Less," Mark Manson, accessed August 21, 2021, https://markmanson.net/how-to-be-more-productive.

2. "Immanuel Kant," Goodreads, accessed July 14, 2021, https://www.goodreads .com/quotes/1250366-from-such-crooked-wood-as-that-which-man-is-made.

3. Michelle Chapman, "Amazon's Growth Continues in 2021, More Jobs to Boston," ABC News, January 26, 2021, https://abcnews.go.com/Business/wireStory /amazons-growth-continues-2021-jobs-boston-75487027.

4. Justin Bariso, "Jeff Bezos Schedules His Most Important Meetings at 10 a.m. Here's Why You Should Too," *Inc.*, September 17, 2018, https://www.inc .com/justin-bariso/jeff-bezos-schedules-his-most-important-meetings-before -lunch-heres-why-you-should-too.html.

5. Matt Perman, *What's Best Next: How the Gospel Transforms the Way You Get Things Done* (Grand Rapids: Zondervan, 2016), 196–97.

6. Tim Ferriss, "Neil Gaiman—The Interview I've Waited 20 Years to Do," *Tim Ferriss Show* (blog), March 28, 2019, https://tim.blog/2019/03/28/neil-gaiman/.

7. Perman, *What's Best Next*, 211.

8. Lisa Feldman Barrett, phone interview with author, July 17, 2020, transcript and audio recording available.

9. Barrett, interview.

10. Keller and Papasan, *The ONE Thing*, 66.

Chapter 3 Capture the Hope Moments

1. Nir Eyal, phone interview with author, July 17, 2020, transcript and audio recording available.

2. Charles Duhigg, *Smarter Faster Better: The Transformative Power of Real Productivity* (New York: Random House, 2016), 132.

Chapter 4 Put Yourself on the Right Path

1. Stephen J. Dubner and Angela Duckworth, "How Do You Know When It's Time to Quit?," *No Stupid Questions* podcast, Freakonomics, November 29, 2020, https://freakonomics.com/podcast/nsq-quitting/.

2. Bill Bryson, *The Body: A Guide for Occupants* (New York: Knopf Doubleday, 2019), 147.

3. Marshall Goldsmith, *Triggers: Creating Behavior That Lasts—Becoming the Person You Want to Be* (New York: Crown Business, 2015), 185.

4. Jordan Peterson, "Jordan Peterson: How To Deal With Depression," You-Tube video, 49:45, posted by "Motivation Madness," February 25, 2018, https://www.youtube.com/watch?v=Xm_2zmX6Akc.

5. John Brandon, "Science Says There's a Simple Reason You Keep Thinking Negative Thoughts All Day," *Inc.*, September 16, 2019, https://www.inc.com/john-brandon/science-says-theres-a-simple-reason-you-keep-thinking-negative-thoughts-all-day.html.

6. Brandon, "Science Says There's a Simple Reason You Keep Thinking Negative Thoughts All Day."

Chapter 5 Learn How to Focus

1. John Mark Comer, *The Ruthless Elimination of Hurry: How to Stay Emotionally Healthy and Spiritually Alive in the Chaos of the Modern World* (Colorado Springs: WaterBrook, 2019), 121.

2. Microsoft ad, YouTube video, 1:08, posted by "Microsoft 365," April 19, 2017, https://www.youtube.com/watch?v=6k3_T84z5Ds.

3. G. Lindgaard, G. Fernandes, C. Dudek, and J. Brown, "Attention Web Designers: You Have 50 Milliseconds to Make a Good First Impression!," ResearchGate, accessed April 14, 2021, https://www.researchgate.net/publication/220208334_Attention_web_designers_You_have_50_milliseconds_to_make_a_good_first_impression_Behaviour_and_Information_Technology_252_115–126.

4. Comer, *The Ruthless Elimination of Hurry*, 94.

5. Tim Ferriss, *Tribe of Mentors: Short Life Advice from the Best in the World* (Boston: Houghton Mifflin Harcourt, 2017), 205.

6. John Brandon, "Where You Focus Will Become Your Greatest Area of Success. Here's Why," *Inc.*, April 29, 2016, https://www.inc.com/john-brandon/where-you-focus-will-become-your-greatest-area-of-success-heres-why.html.

7. Ryan Holiday, *The Obstacle Is the Way: The Timeless Art of Turning Trials into Triumph* (London: Portfolio, 2014).

8. Tania Lombrozo, "This Could Have Been Shorter," NPR, February 3, 2014, https://www.npr.org/sections/13.7/2014/02/03/270680304/this-could-have-been-shorter.

9. Laura Vanderkam, *The New Corner Office: How the Most Successful People Work from Home* (London: Portfolio, 2020), chap. 2, Kindle.

10. Jordan Raynor, Zoom interview with author, February 25, 2021, transcript and audio recording available.

11. Gretchen Rubin, "There Is No More Miserable Human Being Than One in Whom Nothing Is Habitual," *Gretchen Rubin* (blog), July 13, 2014, https://gretchenrubin.com/2014/07/there-is-no-more-miserable-human-being-than-one-in-whom-nothing-is-habitual.

12. Ryan Holiday, *Stillness Is the Key*, 225.

13. Holiday, *Stillness Is the Key*, 259.

Chapter 6 Stop Relying So Much on Lists

1. "About Me," Rahul Vohra, accessed April 15, 2021, https://about.me/rahulvohra.

2. Rahul Vohra, phone interview with author, September 19, 2020, transcript and audio recording available.

3. Barrett, interview.

4. Shane O'Mara, *In Praise of Walking: A New Scientific Exploration* (New York: Norton, 2019), 148.

5. James Clear, *Atomic Habits: Tiny Changes, Remarkable Results: An Easy & Proven Way to Build Good Habits & Break Bad Ones* (London: Penguin, 2018), 165.

6. James Clear, "How Long Does It Actually Take to Form a New Habit? (Backed by Science)," James Clear, accessed April 15, 2021, https://jamesclear.com/new-habit.

7. Alyssa Satara, "In 1 Sentence Arianna Huffington Captured the Pathway to Success," *Inc.*, February 27, 2018, https://www.inc.com/alyssa-satara/arianna-huffington-said-this-1-thing-showed-us-how-to-get-closer-to-success.html.

8. Charles Duhigg, *The Power of Habit* (New York: Random House, 2012), 276.

9. Clear, *Atomic Habits*, 203.

10. Duhigg, *The Power of Habit*, 100.

11. Duhigg, *The Power of Habit*, 273.

Chapter 7 Do the Most Important Tasks First

1. Walker Meade, "Every Breath You Take," *Herald Tribune*, January 12, 2010, https://www.heraldtribune.com/article/LK/20100112/News/605199447/SH.

2. James Young, "Heroes of Employee Engagement: No. 4 Edwin A. Locke," *Peakon* (blog), December 13, 2017, https://peakon.com/us/blog/future-work/edwin-locke-goal-setting-theory/.

3. Ryder Carroll, phone interview with author, September 19, 2020, transcript and audio recording available.

4. James Clear, "The Myth of Multitasking: Why Fewer Priorities Leads to Better Work," James Clear, accessed April 15, 2021, https://jamesclear.com/multitasking-myth; Keller and Papasan, *The ONE Thing*, 47.

5. Matt Plummer, "Interruptions Steal a Ton of Your Time. Here Are 3 Ways to Get Those Hours Back," *Inc.*, January 30, 2019, https://www.inc.com/matt

-plummer/interruptions-steal-a-ton-of-your-time-here-are-3-ways-to-get
-those-hours-back.html.

6. Keller and Papasan, *The ONE Thing*, 47.

7. Bruce Davis, "There Are 50,000 Thoughts Standing Between You and Your Partner Every Day!," HuffPost, updated July 23, 2013, https://www.huffpost.com /entry/healthy-relationships_b_3307916.

8. Keller and Papasan, *The ONE Thing*, 47.

9. "Multitasking: Switching Costs," American Psychological Association, March 20, 2006, https://www.apa.org/research/action/multitask; Keller and Papasan, *The ONE Thing*, 48.

10. Douglas Martin, "Wayne E. Oates, 82, Is Dead; Coined the Term 'Workaholic,'" *New York Times*, October 26, 1999, https://www.nytimes.com/1999/10 /26/us/wayne-e-oates-82-is-dead-coined-the-term-workaholic.html.

11. "9,000 Years of Sipping: The History of Alcoholism," Shoreline Recovery Center, accessed April 15, 2021, https://shorelinerecoverycenter.com/9000-years -of-sipping-the-history-of-alcoholism/.

12. Keller and Papasan, *The ONE Thing*, 80.

13. Katherine Meikle, "How Does Overworking Affect Physical and Mental Health?," Passport Health, February 2019, https://www.passporthealthusa .com/employer-solutions/blog/2019-2-overworking-affect-physical-and-mental -health/.

14. Keller and Papasan, *The ONE Thing*, 193.

15. "Slow Hack 007: Say 'NO' Often to Say 'YES' to What Matters," Sloww, June 6, 2018, https://medium.com/@slowwco/slow-hack-007-say-no-often-to -say-yes-to-what-matters-b943a478585.

16. Ryder Carroll, phone interview with author, August 3, 2020, transcript and audio recording available.

17. Frank Herron, "It's a MUCH More Effective Quotation to Attribute It to Aristotle, Rather than to Will Durant," UMass Boston blog, May 8, 2012, https://blogs.umb.edu/quoteunquote/2012/05/08/its-a-much-more-effective -quotation-to-attribute-it-to-aristotle-rather-than-to-will-durant/.

Chapter 8 How to Set Critical Goals

1. John Brandon, "Here's My Plan: I Don't Ever Want to Use Zoom Again," *Forbes*, June 24, 2020, https://www.forbes.com/sites/johnbbrandon/2020/06 /24/heres-my-plan-i-dont-ever-want-to-use-zoom-again.

2. Alan Henry, "Marissa Mayer Explains Why Having To-Dos Is Better Than Finishing Them," LifeHacker, December 10, 2013, https://lifehacker.com/marissa -mayer-explains-why-having-to-dos-is-better-than-1480109287.

3. Chris Bailey, "The Biggest Productivity Mistake You've Never Heard Of— And Why So Many People Are Guilty of It Every Day," *Make It* (blog), July 30, 2020, https://www.cnbc.com/2020/07/30/biggest-productivity-mistake-most -people-dont-know-they-make-every-day-work-expert.html.

4. Kendra Adachi, *The Lazy Genius Way: Embrace What Matters, Ditch What Doesn't, and Get Stuff Done* (Austin: Waterbrook, 2020), 18.

5. Adachi, *The Lazy Genius Way*, 12.

6. Rebecca Mead, "All about the Hamiltons," *New Yorker*, February 2, 2015, https://www.newyorker.com/magazine/2015/02/09/hamiltons.

Chapter 9 How to Avoid Decision Fatigue

1. Walter Isaacson, *Steve Jobs: The Exclusive Biography* (New York: Simon & Schuster, 2011), 362.

2. Nir Eyal, "Have We Been Thinking about Willpower the Wrong Way for 30 Years?," November 23, 2016, *Harvard Business Review*, https://hbr.org/2016/11/have-we-been-thinking-about-willpower-the-wrong-way-for-30-years.

3. John Tierney, "Do You Suffer from Decision Fatigue?," *New York Times Magazine*, August 21, 2011, https://www.nytimes.com/2011/08/21/magazine/do-you-suffer-from-decision-fatigue.html.

4. Daniel Pink, *When: The Scientific Secrets of Perfect Timing* (New York: Penguin Random House, 2018), 58–61.

5. Pink, *When*, 61.

6. Pink, *When*, 61.

7. Pink, *When*, 61.

8. Pink, *When*, 62.

9. Melanie Curtin, "In an 8-Hour Day, the Average Worker Is Productive for This Many Hours," *Inc.*, July 21, 2016, https://www.inc.com/melanie-curtin/in-an-8-hour-day-the-average-worker-is-productive-for-this-many-hours.html.

10. BJ Fogg, "Motivation Wave," YouTube video, 22:55, posted by "Dr. BJ Fogg," April 15, 2012, https://www.youtube.com/watch?v=fqUSjHjIEFg.

11. Brendon Burchard, *High Performance Habits: How Extraordinary People Become that Way* (Carlsbad, CA: Hay House, 2017), 185.

12. Burchard, *High Performance Habits*, 186.

13. Jefferson Bethke, *To Hell with the Hustle: Reclaiming Your Life in an Overworked, Overspent, and Overconnected World* (Nashville: Thomas Nelson, 2019), 81.

14. Alex Soojung-Kim Pang, "Arianna Huffington on a Book About Working Less, Resting More," *The New York Times*, December 12, 2016, https://www.nytimes.com/2016/12/12/books/review/arianna-huffington-rest-alex-soojung-kim-pang.html.

15. "Ford Factory Workers Get 40-Hour Week," History, last updated April 29, 2020, https://www.history.com/this-day-in-history/ford-factory-workers-get-40-hour-week; and Michael Hyatt, *Free to Focus: A Total Productivity System to Achieve More by Doing Less* (Grand Rapids: Baker Books, 2019), 38–39.

16. "Tork Survey Reveals Lunch Break Impact on Workplace," Tork, May 16, 2018, https://www.torkusa.com/about/pressroom/tbtlb.

Chapter 10 Stop Tunneling Your Goals

1. Mary Dodson Wade, *Christopher Columbus: Famous Explorer* (Mankato, MN: Capstone Press, 2007).

2. Jace Larson, "Christopher Columbus's Early Influences and Experiences," Julesburg Advocate, updated April 24, 2019, https://www.julesburgadvocate.com/2010/04/30/christopher-columbuss-early-influences-and-experiences.

3. "Columbus Day," Library of Congress, accessed April 19, 2021, https://www.loc.gov/item/today-in-history/october-12/.

4. "Why Columbus Day Courts Controversy," History, updated October 9, 2020, https://www.history.com/news/columbus-day-controversy.

5. Ricky Rusting, "Will the Real Christopher Columbus Please Stand Up?," *Scientific American*, October 14, 2013, https://blogs.scientificamerican.com/anecdotes-from-the-archive/will-the-real-christopher-columbus-please-stand-up/.

6. Alison Eldridge, "5 Unbelievable Facts about Christopher Columbus," *Encyclopaedia Britannica Online*, accessed April 19, 2021, https://www.britannica.com/list/5-unbelievable-facts-about-christopher-columbus.

7. Valerie I. J. Flint, "Christopher Columbus," Britannica, last updated April 8, 2021, https://www.britannica.com/biography/Christopher-Columbus.

8. Sandipan Deb, "Christopher Columbus, the Murderer," Mint, updated September 16, 2017, https://www.livemint.com/Sundayapp/23nihEItoCYOAdHZ0y7JxK/Christopher-Columbus-the-murderer.html.

9. "Columbus Reaches the 'New World,'" History, updated October 12, 2020, https://www.history.com/this-day-in-history/columbus-reaches-the-new-world.

10. Philip VanDusen, "How to Be Happier and More Productive—Does Time Management Eliminate Spontaneity?," YouTube video, 5:41, posted by "Philip VanDusen," February 17, 2020, https://www.youtube.com/watch?v=Ht2Xh7XtczE.

11. John Eldredge, *Get Your Life Back: Everyday Practices for a World Gone Mad* (Nashville: Thomas Nelson, 2020), 25.

12. Barrett, interview.

13. VanDusen, "How to Be Happier and More Productive."

14. Dan Heath, *Upstream: The Quest to Solve Problems Before They Happen* (New York: Avid Reader Press, 2020), 60.

15. Heath, *Upstream*, 59.

16. Bethke, *To Hell with the Hustle*, 12.

17. Amitava Chattopadhyay, Antonios Stamatogiannakis, and Dipanar Chakravarti, "Why You Should Stop Setting Easy Goals," *Harvard Business Review*, November 27, 2018, https://hbr.org/2018/11/why-you-should-stop-setting-easy-goals.

18. Adachi, *The Lazy Genius Way*, 45.

Chapter 11 Becoming More Self-Aware

1. Mark Batterson, *Whisper: How to Hear the Voice of God* (New York: Crown Publishing, 2020), 133.

2. "Napoleon Hill," Your Dictionary, accessed April 29, 2021, https://quotes.yourdictionary.com/author/napoleon-hill/62772.

3. Rich Roll, "Digital Minimalism with Cal Newport," *Rich Roll* podcast, June 10, 2019, https://www.youtube.com/watch?v=9L-Uoo4Vrlk.

Chapter 12 Achieving Goals by Unlearning Old Habits

1. Bob Hartman, "Peter Drucker Understood Agile Leadership and Agility before It Even Existed!," Agile for All, November 16, 2015, https://agileforall.com/peter-drucker-understood-agile-leadership-and-agility-before-it-even-existed/.

2. John Brandon, "A Computer Controlled by Hand Gestures," *Inc.*, February 1, 2011, https://www.inc.com/magazine/20110201/a-computer-controlled-by-hand-gestures.html.

3. Filiberto Fuentenebro de Diego and Carmen Valiente Ots, "Nostalgia: A Conceptual History," Sage Journals, November 13, 2014, https://journals.sagepub.com/doi/10.1177/0957154X14545290.

4. For "twenty thousand breaths," see Brown, "How Many Breaths Do You Take Each Day?"; for "fifty thousand thoughts," see Davis, "There Are 50,000 Thoughts Standing Between You and Your Partner Every Day!"

5. "Neale Donald Walsch," Pass It On, accessed April 20, 2021, https://www.passiton.com/inspirational-quotes/7568-the-struggle-ends-when-gratitude-begins.

6. John Brandon, "Science Says There's a Simple Reason You Keep Thinking Negative Thoughts All Day."

7. "Henry David Thoreau," Goodreads, accessed July 14, 2021, https://www.goodreads.com/quotes/7426074-it-s-not-what-you-look-at-that-matters-it-s-what.

8. Mark Buchanan, *God Walk: Moving at the Speed of Your Soul* (Grand Rapids: Zondervan, 2020), 47.

Chapter 13 Hardship Makes Us Stronger

1. Ferriss, *Tribe of Mentors*, 26.

2. Henry Ford, Goodreads, accessed July 14, 2021, https://www.goodreads.com/quotes/24623-obstacles-are-those-frightful-things-you-see-when-you-take.

3. Ferriss, *Tribe of Mentors*, 228.

4. Louis L'Amour, *Lonely on the Mountain* (New York: Random House, 2003), 1.

5. Tom Brady interview, *Armchair Expert* podcast, accessed April 20, 2021, https://armchairexpertpod.com/pods/tom-brady.

Chapter 14 Ending the Day with Renewed Hope

1. Hyatt, *Free to Focus*, 50.

2. Hyatt, *Free to Focus*, 84–85.

3. Barrett, interview.

4. Nir Eyal, *Indistractable: How to Control Your Attention and Choose Your Life* (Dallas: BenBella Books, 2019), 13.

5. Holiday, *Stillness Is the Key*, 32.

6. Jordan Raynor, *Redeeming Your Time: 7 Biblical Principles for Being Purposeful, Present, and Wildly Productive* (Colorado Springs: WaterBrook, forthcoming).

7. Burchard, *High Performance Habits*, 179.

8. Holiday, *Stillness Is the Key*, 120.

9. Chuck Swindoll, "It's Only Money," Insights for Living, archive video, accessed April 20, 2021, https://www.insight.org/resources/video-library/individual/175/its-only-money.

Chapter 15 Houston, We Have an Email Problem

1. James Veitch, "This Is What Happens When You Reply to Spam Email," TED, December 2015, https://www.ted.com/talks/james_veitch_this_is_what_happens_when_you_reply_to_spam_email.

2. Joseph Johnson, "Number of E-Mails Per Day Worldwide 2017–2025," Statista, April 7, 2021, https://www.statista.com/statistics/456500/daily-number-of-e-mails-worldwide/.

3. "Immanuel Kant," StriveZen, accessed July 14, 2021, https://www.strivezen.com/wisdom-is-organized-life/.

4. C. S. Lewis, *The Screwtape Letters* (New York: HarperCollins, 2001), 138.

5. Jocelyn K. Glei, *Unsubscribe: How to Kill Email Anxiety, Avoid Distractions, and Get Real Work Done* (New York: PublicAffairs, 2016), 5.

6. James Clear, "Warren Buffett's '2 List' Strategy: How to Maximize Your Focus and Master Your Priorities," James Clear, accessed April 21, 2021, https://jamesclear.com/buffett-focus.

7. David Allen, *Getting Things Done: The Art of Stress-Free Productivity* (New York: Penguin, 2015), 136.

8. Cal Newport, "A Productivity Lesson from a Classic Arcade Game," *Study Hacks Blog*, September 6, 2016, https://www.calnewport.com/blog/2016/09/06/a-productivity-lesson-from-a-classic-arcade-game/.

9. Linda Stone, "Are You Breathing? Do You Have Email Apnea?," Linda Stone, accessed April 21, 2021, https://lindastone.net/2014/11/24/are-you-breathing-do-you-have-email-apnea/.

10. John Brandon, "How a Digital Detox Changed My Tech Habits," Fox News, last updated November 4, 2015, https://www.foxnews.com/tech/how-a-digital-detox-changed-my-tech-habits.

11. John Ortberg, *Eternity Is Now in Session: A Radical Rediscovery of What Jesus Really Taught about Salvation, Eternity, and Getting to the Good Place* (Carol Stream, IL: Tyndale, 2018), 100.

Chapter 16 Reclaim Thirty Hours of Work

1. John Brandon, "Why Email Will Be Obsolete by 2020," *Inc.*, April 16, 2015, https://www.inc.com/john-brandon/why-email-will-be-obsolete-by-2020.html.

2. Wayne Kurtzman, phone interview and email with author, July 3, 2020.

3. Geoffrey James, "New Study: The Average Worker Spends 30 Hours a Week Checking Email," *Inc.*, August 27, 2015, https://www.inc.com/geoffrey-james/new-study-the-average-worker-spends-30-hours-a-week-checking-email.html.

4. Cal Newport, *A World Without Email* (New York: Penguin, 2021).

5. Chris Bailey, *Hyperfocus: How to Be More Productive in a World of Distraction* (New York: Penguin, 2018), 41.

6. Hyatt, *Free to Focus*, 13.

7. Jennifer J. Deal, "Welcome to the 72-Hour Work Week," *Harvard Business Review*, September 12, 2013, https://hbr.org/2013/09/welcome-to-the-72-hour-work-we.

8. Roll, "Digital Minimalism with Cal Newport."

9. Neal Stephenson, "Why I Am a Bad Correspondent," Neal Stephenson, accessed April 29, 2021, https://www.nealstephenson.com/why-i-am-a-bad-correspondent.html.

10. John Brandon, "The Survey Results Are In: Millennials Hate Boomers," *Inc.*, April 28, 2018, https://www.inc.com/john-brandon/the-survey-results-just -came-in-millennials-hate-boomers-just-as-much-as-we-thought.html.

Chapter 17 The Great Email Challenge

1. Katie Notopoulos, "I Tried Emailing Like a CEO and Quite Frankly, It Made My Life Better," BuzzFeed News, November 30, 2017, https://www.buzzfeednews .com/article/katienotopoulos/i-tried-emailing-like-your-boss.

2. Eyal, *Indistractable*, 90–91.

3. Cal Newport, "Was E-Mail a Mistake?," *New Yorker*, August 6, 2019, https:// www.newyorker.com/tech/annals-of-technology/was-e-mail-a-mistake.

4. Cal Newport, "Our Brains Are Not Multi-Threaded," *Study Hacks Blog*, September 10, 2019, https://www.calnewport.com/blog/2019/09/10/our-brains -are-not-multi-threaded/.

5. Teresa M. Amabile and Steven J. Kramer, "The Power of Small Wins," *Harvard Business Review*, May 2011, https://hbr.org/2011/05/the-power-of-small-wins.

6. Glei, *Unsubscribe*, 11.

7. Glei, *Unsubscribe*, 8.

8. *The Social Dilemma*, directed by Jeff Orlowski, Netflix, 2020, https://www .netflix.com/title/81254224.

9. *The Social Dilemma*.

Chapter 18 The Real Goal Is Relationships

1. Hyatt, *Free to Focus*, 191–94.

2. Hyatt, *Free to Focus*, 241.

3. Raynor, *Redeeming Your Time*, forthcoming.

4. Holiday, *Stillness Is the Key*, 34.

5. "Marcus Aurelius," Goodreads, accessed April 21, 2021, https://www .goodreads.com/quotes/7998994-ask-yourself-at-every-moment-is-this-neces sary.

6. Comer, *The Ruthless Elimination of Hurry*, 230.

7. Drake Baer, "Dwight Eisenhower Nailed a Major Insight about Productivity," *Business Insider*, April 10, 2014, https://www.businessinsider.com/dwight -eisenhower-nailed-a-major-insight-about-productivity.

Chapter 19 The Great Deception

1. Nicholas Carr, *The Shallows: What the Internet Is Doing to Our Brains* (New York: W. W. Norton & Company, 2011).

2. Kris Reid, "11 Search Statistics You Need to Know in 2021," Ardor SEO, accessed April 21, 2021, https://ardorseo.com/blog/how-many-google-searches -per-day/.

3. "Internet 2010 in Numbers," Solarwinds Pingdom, January 12, 2011, https:// www.pingdom.com/blog/internet-2010-in-numbers.

4. Matt Ahlgren, "100+ Internet Statistics and Facts for 2021," W, updated March 23, 2021, https://www.websitehostingrating.com/internet-statistics-facts.

5. Carr, *The Shallows*, "Introduction."

6. Eldredge, *Get Your Life Back*, 41.

7. Carr, *The Shallows*, 227.

8. "Thomas A. Edison," Goodreads, accessed July 14, 2021, https://www
.goodreads.com/quotes/7331844-being-busy-does-not-always-mean-real-work
-the-object.

9. Hyatt, *Free to Focus*, 14.

10. "Abraham Joshua Heschel," Goodreads, accessed April 22, 2012, https://
www.goodreads.com/quotes/30322-never-once-in-my-life-did-i-ask-god-for.

11. Daniela Di Noi, "Do Workers Still Waste Time Searching for Information?," *Xenit Blog*, May 22, 2018, https://blog.xenit.eu/blog/do-workers-still
-waste-time-searching-for-information.

12. Di Noi, "Do Workers Still Waste Time Searching for Information?"

13. Cal Newport, phone interview with author, October 26, 2020, transcript
and audio recording available.

Chapter 20 What Happens to Your Brain When You Surf

1. Deyan Georgiev, "101+ Google Statistics and Facts that Reveal Everything
about the Tech Giant," Review 42, last updated February 19, 2021, https://re
view42.com/google-statistics-and-facts.

2. *The Social Dilemma*.

3. David Morgan, "Former Silicon Valley Insider on How Technology Is
'Downgrading Humans,'" *CBS This Morning*, May 6, 2019, https://www.cbsnews
.com/news/former-silicon-valley-insider-on-how-technology-is-downgrading
-humans/.

4. Mike Allen, "Sean Parker Unloads on Facebook: 'God Only Knows What It's
Doing to Our Children's Brains,'" Axios, November 9, 2017, https://www.axios
.com/sean-parker-unloads-on-facebook-god-only-knows-what-its-doing-to-our
-childrens-brains-1513306792-f855e7b4-4e99-4d60-8d51-2775559c2671.html.

5. James Vincent, "Former Facebook exec says social media is ripping apart
society," The Verge, December 11, 2017, https://www.theverge.com/2017/12/11
/16761016/former-facebook-exec-ripping-apart-society.

6. Bill Snyder, "Chamath Palihapitiya: Why Failing Fast Fails," Stanford Business, December 12, 2017, https://www.gsb.stanford.edu/insights/chamath-pa
lihapitiya-why-failing-fast-fails.

7. "Landmark Report: U.S. Teens Use an Average of Nine Hours of Media Per
Day, Tweens Use Six Hours," Common Sense Media, November 3, 2015, https://
www.commonsensemedia.org/about-us/news/press-releases/landmark-report
-us-teens-use-an-average-of-nine-hours-of-media-per-day.

8. "Why & How Your Employees Are Wasting Time at Work," Salary.com,
accessed April 22, 2021, https://www.salary.com/articles/why-how-your-employ
ees-are-wasting-time-at-work/.

9. Leo Yeykelis, "Switching Every 19 Seconds: How Our Brains Multitask
with New Media," April 4, 2018, https://www.forbes.com/sites/leoyeykelis
/2018/04/04/switching-every-19-seconds-how-our-brains-multitask-with
-new-media.

10. John Brandon, "Forget Banning Phones and Laptops at Meetings. Here's What We Should Ban Instead," *Inc.*, October 13, 2018, https://www.inc.com /john-brandon/forget-banning-phones-laptops-at-meetings-heres-what-we -should-ban-instead.html.

11. John Brandon, "MIT Expert to Office Workers: Set Your Phones Down and Let's Talk," *Inc.*, October 15, 2015, https://www.inc.com/john-brandon/mit -expert-to-office-workers-set-your-phones-down-and-let-s-talk.html.

12. Aviv M. Weinstein, "An Update Overview on Brain Imaging Studies of Internet Gaming Disorder," NCBI, September 29, 2017, https://www.ncbi.nlm .nih.gov/pmc/articles/PMC5626837/.

13. Bethke, *To Hell with the Hustle*, 10; and M. G. Siegler, "Eric Schmidt: Every 2 Days We Create as Much Information as We Did Up to 2003," Tech Crunch, August 4, 2010, https://techcrunch.com/2010/08/04/schmidt-data/.

14. Adam Alter, *Irresistible: The Rise of Addictive Technology and the Business of Keeping Us Hooked* (London: Penguin, 2018), 68.

15. John Brandon, "Is Technology Making Us Less Human?," TechRadar, August 6, 2013, https://www.techradar.com/news/world-of-tech/future-tech /is-technology-making-us-less-human-1171002.

16. *Driveways*, directed by Andrew Ahn, produced by Maven Pictures, released February 10, 2019.

Chapter 21 Feeding the Right Wolf When You're Online

1. Timothy Ferriss, *The 4-Hour Workweek: Escape 9–5, Live Anywhere, and Join the New Rich* (New York: Crown Publishing, 2009).

2. Samuel Thomas Davies, "*Essentialism* by Greg McKeown," Sam T. Davies, accessed April 22, 2021, https://www.samuelthomasdavies.com/book-summaries /business/essentialism/.

3. Evan Travers, "Review: *Essentialism* by Greg McKeown," *Evan Travers* (blog), September 1, 2019, http://evantravers.com/articles/2019/09/01/review-essen tialism-by-greg-mckeown.

4. Gretchen Rubin, "Now Is Now. It Can Never Be a Long Time Ago," *Gretchen Rubin* (blog), January 11, 2014, https://gretchenrubin.com/2014/01/now-is-now -it-can-never-be-a-long-time-ago/.

5. "Marcus Aurelius," Goodreads, accessed April 22, 2021, https://www.goodreads .com/quotes/3860316-concentrate-every-minute-like-a-roman-like-a-man-on.

6. Snyder, "Chamath Palihapitiya."

7. Terra Boake, "Digital 2020," We Are Social, January 30, 2020, https:// wearesocial.com/ca/2020/01/30/digital-2020-what-you-really-need-to-know/.

8. Alex Hern, "Netflix's Biggest Competitor? Sleep," *The Guardian*, April 18, 2017, https://www.theguardian.com/technology/2017/apr/18/netflix-competi tor-sleep-uber-facebook.

Chapter 22 Avoiding the Doom Scroll on Social Media

1. Lisa S. Mataloni, "GDP and the Economy," SCB, August 2019, https://apps .bea.gov/scb/2019/08-august/0819-gdp-economy.htm.

2. Roxanna Edwards and Sean M. Smith, "Job Market Remains Tight in 2019, as the Unemployment Rate Falls to Its Lowest Level Since 1969," U.S. Bureau of Labor Statistics, April 2020, https://www.bls.gov/opub/mlr/2020/article/job -market-remains-tight-in-2019-as-the-unemployment-rate-falls-to-its-lowest -level-since-1969.htm.

3. Nir Eyal, "Infinite Scroll: The Web's Slot Machine," Nir and Far, accessed April 22, 2021, https://www.nirandfar.com/the-webs-slot-machine/.

4. "Employment Situation Summary Table A. Household Data," US Bureau of Labor Statistics, last modified April 2, 2021, https://www.bls.gov/news.release /empsit.a.htm.

5. "Gross Domestic Product, 2nd Quarter 2020," US Bureau of Economic Analysis, last modified August 18, 2020, https://www.bea.gov/news/2020/gross -domestic-product-2nd-quarter-2020-advance-estimate-and-annual-update.

6. Nir Eyal, phone interview with author, July 17, 2020, transcript and audio recording available.

7. David Sayce, "The Number of Tweets per Day in 2020," David Sayce, accessed April 22, 2021, https://www.dsayce.com/social-media/tweets-day.

8. "We Wake Up Happy, Have a Miserable Day, but Cheer Up in the Evening: How Twitter Tracks Our Moods," *Daily Mail*, September 30, 2011, https://www .dailymail.co.uk/sciencetech/article-2043606/Twitter-analysis-shows-positive -thing-morning.html.

9. Mike Maughan, "Using Behavioral Science to Help Parents Navigate a New Reality," Thrive Global, May 14, 2020, https://thriveglobal.com/stories/be haviloral-science-help-parents-work-from-home-family-lessons/.

10. Michael Miller, "Addicted to Your Smartphone? Not So Fast," Six-Seconds, January 8, 2019, https://www.6seconds.org/2020/01/06/become -indistractable.

11. Comer, *The Ruthless Elimination of Hurry*, 185.

12. *The Social Dilemma*.

13. Center for Humane Technology, "Are the Kids Alright?," *Your Undivided Attention* podcast, October 27, 2020, https://www.humanetech.com/podcast /26-are-the-kids-alright.

14. "Americans Check Their Phones 96 Times a Day," Asurion, November 21, 2019, https://www.asurion.com/about/press-releases/americans-check-their -phones-96-times-a-day.

Chapter 23 The Hyperactive Hivemind of Online Obsession

1. Roll, "Digital Minimalism with Cal Newport."

2. Tea Romih, "Humans Are Visual Creatures," Seyens, October 12, 2016, https://www.seyens.com/humans-are-visual-creatures/.

3. Mark R. Leary, "Sociometer Theory and the Pursuit of Relational Value: Getting to the Root of Self-Esteem," Taylor & Francis Online, March 4, 2011, https://www.tandfonline.com/doi/abs/10.1080/10463280540000007.

4. Emily Gould, "How Much My Novel Cost Me," Human Parts, February 24, 2014, https://humanparts.medium.com/how-much-my-novel-cost-me -35d7c8aec846.

Chapter 24 The Relentless Pursuit of Perfection

1. Jaron Lanier, *Ten Arguments for Deleting Your Social Media Accounts Right Now* (New York: Henry Holt, 2018), 15.

2. Comer, *The Ruthless Elimination of Hurry*, 27.

3. Eldredge, *Get Your Life Back*, xii.

4. Eldredge, *Get Your Life Back*, xiii.

5. Eldredge, *Get Your Life Back*, xv.

6. Saima Salim, "More Than Six Hours of Our Day Is Spent Online—Digital 2019 Report," Digital Information World, February 4, 2019, https://www.digital informationworld.com/2019/02/internet-users-spend-more-than-a-quarter-of -their-lives-online.html.

7. "Henry David Thoreau," Goodreads, accessed July 14, 2021, https:// www.goodreads.com/quotes/7273089-it-s-not-enough-to-be-busy-so-are -the-ants.

Chapter 25 Selling an Idea in Only Seven Minutes

1. Medienwandel, "Macworld 1997: The Return of Steve Jobs," YouTube video, 38:31, posted by "medienwandel," October 19, 2011, https://www.youtube.com /watch?v=lOs6hnT14lw.

2. "Apple Market Cap 2006–2020," Macrotrends, accessed April 27, 2021, https://www.macrotrends.net/stocks/charts/AAPL/apple/market-cap.

3. Jack Nicas, "Apple Reaches 2 Trillion, Punctuating Big Tech's Grip," *New York Times*, August 19, 2020, https://www.nytimes.com/2020/08/19/technology /apple-2-trillion.html.

Chapter 26 How Sustained Attention Span Works

1. "Why PowerPoint Presentations Always Die after 10 Minutes and How to Rescue Them," Enterprise Florida, April 30, 2014, https://www.forbes.com/sites /carminegallo/2014/04/30/why-powerpoint-presentations-always-die-after-10 -minutes-and-how-to-rescue-them.

2. For Dale Carnegie biographical information, see the following: Dale Carnegie, "Our Proof is in Our History," Dale Carnegie, accessed August 21, 2021, https://www.dalecarnegie.com/en/approach/heritage; Biography.com Editors, "Dale Carnegie," The Biography.com Website, April 15, 2019, https://www.bio graphy.com/writer/dale-carnegie; Harlem World Magazine, "Carnegie Discovered 'How To Win Friends And Influence People' In Harlem, 1911," Harlem World Magazine, November 26, 2017, https://www.harlemworldmagazine.com/dale -carnegie-discovered-win-friends-influence-people-harlem-1911/; Dan Coffey, "Carnegie, Dale (1888-1955)," Encyclopedia.com, Updated August 17, 2021, https:// www.encyclopedia.com/media/encyclopedias-almanacs-transcripts-and-maps /carnegie-dale-1888-1955.

3. Veitch, "This Is What Happens When You Reply to Spam Email."

4. Geoffrey James, "Jeff Bezos Banned PowerPoint and It's Arguably the Smartest Management Move He's Ever Made," *Inc.*, accessed April 27, 2021, https://

www.inc.com/geoffrey-james/jeff-bezos-banned-powerpoint-its-arguably
-smartest-management-move-that-hes-ever-made.html.

5. Robert C. Pozen, *Extreme Productivity: Boost Your Results, Reduce Your Hours* (New York: Harper Business, 2012), 93.

6. Vineet Arya, "How Not to Lose Attention of Gen Z in the 8 Seconds that You Have?," *Entrepreneur*, June 5, 2019, https://www.entrepreneur.com/article /334791.

Chapter 27 Closing the Deal in Your Presentation

1. Brittany Thoms, phone interview with author, November 23, 2020, transcript and audio recording available.

2. Peter Drucker, Goodreads, accessed July 14, 2021, https://www.goodreads .com/quotes/31286-efficiency-is-doing-the-thing-right-effectiveness-is-doing-the.

3. Nancy Duarte, "The Secret Structure of Great Talks," TED, November 2011, https://www.ted.com/talks/nancy_duarte_the_secret_structure_of_great _talks.

Chapter 28 Why the Best Meetings Are Short

1. Joakim Stattin, "5 Quotes about Masterfully Effective Meetings by the World's Top Business Influencers," Stratsys, accessed April 29, 2021, https:// www.stratsys.com/blog/5-quotes-about-masterfully-effective-meetings-by-the -worlds-top-business-influencers.

2. Ryan Shelley, "50 Gary Vaynerchuk Quotes to Get You in Hustle Mode," SMA Marketing, February 18, 2020, https://www.smamarketing.net/blog/gary -vaynerchuk-quotes.

3. "Dave Barry," Goodreads, accessed April 29, 2021, https://www.goodreads .com/quotes/17705-if-you-had-to-identify-in-one-word-the-reason.

4. Amanda Heal, "Don't Make the Mistake of Trying to Accomplish Your Life's Dream Alone," *Purpose Vision Future* (blog), August 8, 2016, https://purpose visionfuture.com/dream-included-need-help-achieve/.

5. Peter Drucker, "Perspective: About Peter Drucker," Drucker Institute, accessed April 29, 2021, https://www.drucker.institute/perspective/about-peter -drucker/.

6. Rahul Vohra, interview.

7. "Herbert A. Simon," Goodreads, accessed April 29, 2021, https://www .goodreads.com/quotes/8502027-in-an-information-rich-world-the-wealth -of-information-means-a.

8. Pozen, *Extreme Productivity*, 85–98.

9. Jessica Stillman, "The Simple Trick Great Thinkers from Charles Darwin to Steve Jobs Used to Be More Creative," *Inc.*, May 29, 2019, https://www.inc .com/jessica-stillman/steve-jobs-swore-by-walking-meetings-heres-science-of -why-theyre-awesome-how-to-do-them-right.html.

10. "Attention in the Classroom: My Best Bets from the Research," *Hobbolog* (blog), January 30, 2020, https://hobbolog.wordpress.com/2020/01/30/attention -in-the-classroom-my-best-bets-from-the-research/.

Chapter 29 Resolve Problems in Seven Minutes

1. Pozen, *Extreme Productivity*, 85–87.

Chapter 30 How to Focus Your Meetings and Your Time

1. Elizabeth Nix, "Did an Apple Really Fall on Isaac Newton's Head?," History, updated September 1, 2018, https://www.history.com/news/did-an-apple-really-fall-on-isaac-newtons-head.

2. McKeown, *Essentialism*, 67.

3. Seth Godin, *This Is Marketing: You Can't Be Seen Until You Learn to See* (London: Penguin, 2018), 46.

John Brandon has lived what he writes about for *Inc.*, *Forbes*, Fox News, and many others. He has a BA in journalism from the University of Northwestern and spent over a decade in the corporate world, becoming director of Information Technology at Best Buy. In the aftermath of corporate restructuring, he traded hats to become a full-time writer/journalist and has published more than 15,000 articles in that time. He and his wife live west of Minneapolis and have four grown children. Learn more at www.sevenminutesolution.com.

CONNECT WITH JOHN

Learn more at
SEVENMINUTESOLUTION.COM